# FINISH LINE

## Writing

### for the Common Core State Standards

Continental

D0315962

# Acknowledgments

**Illustrations:** Page 149: Rob Williams; Page 166: Laurie Conley

**Photographs:** Page 18: PhotoLink; Page 23: www.istockphoto.com/mentaldisorder; Page 24: www.istockphoto.com; Page 27: www.istockphoto.com/Carmen Martínez Banús; Page 33: Library of Congress, Prints and Photographs Division, LC-DIG-bbc-1501f; Page 50: Image used under Creative Commons from Marcin Klapczynski; Page 59: www.istockphoto.com/ZavgSG; Page 76: www.istockphoto.com; Page 85: Nicola Sutton/Life File; Page 95: D.Berry/PhotoLink; Page 118: Stockbyte; Page 141: Image used under Creative Commons by ArtMechanic; Page 158: www.shutterstock.com, Olga Bogatyrenko; Page 195: NASA

ISBN 978-0-8454-6766-4

# Table of Contents

# Welcome to Finish Line Writing for the Common Core State Standards

This book will give you practice in the skills necessary to be an effective writer. It will also help you prepare for writing tests that assess your skills and knowledge.

The material in this book is aligned to the Common Core State Standards for English Language Arts and Literacy in History, Social Studies, Science, and Technical Subjects. The Common Core State Standards (CCSS) build on the education standards developed by the states. The CCSS "specify what literacy skills and understandings are required for college and career readiness in multiple disciplines." This book will help you practice the writing skills necessary to be a literate person in the 21st century.

In the lessons of this book, you will review the writing process and then apply those skills in different types of writing. You will also read informational and literary selections and then answer multiple-choice, short-response, and extended-response questions related to them and to the application of writing skills. The lessons are in three parts:

- The first part introduces the writing skill you are going to study and explains what it is and how you use it.

- The second part is called Guided Practice. You will get more than practice here; you will get help. You will read a nonfiction passage and answer questions about it. After each question, you will find an explanation of the correct answer or a sample answer. So you will answer questions and find out right away if you were correct. You will also learn why one answer is correct and others are not.

- The third part is Test Yourself. Here you will read a question and then write an answer on your own.

After you have finished all of the lessons and units, you will take a Practice Test at the end of the book.

Now you are ready to begin using this book. Good luck!

# Elements of Writing

You probably know a lot about writing. You know it takes thinking and organization. You also know that not all writing is the same. This unit is about the steps in the writing process. It is also about the different types of writing structures.

- **In Lesson 1,** you'll learn about the five steps of the writing process: prewriting, drafting, revising, editing, and publishing. You use this process every time you write.

- **In Lesson 2,** you will find out more about paragraphs. You will review the elements of a paragraph.

- **Lesson 3** is about the main idea and supporting details. You will learn how details help support or explain the main idea. The main idea is what something is about.

- **Lesson 4** shows you how to use cause and effect. This type of structure is best used for events that are related. It helps the reader understand what happened and why it happened.

- **In Lesson 5,** you'll learn how to compare two things. You'll also learn how to contrast two things.

# The Writing Process

**W.3.4–6**

Writing is a process. Most writers follow five steps:

**Prewriting → Drafting → Revising → Editing → Publishing**

An easy way to remember the writing process is to think of what you do in each step. In the prewriting step, you **plan** what you will write. The drafting step is when you actually **write.** Then you go back and **revise** in the revising step. Next, you check, or **edit,** your writing. Finally, you show, or **publish,** your work.

## Step 1: Prewriting

When you plan in the prewriting step, think about these things:

> Read
> Note
> Organize

- Why are you writing? This is called your **purpose.**
- What will you write about? This is called your **subject.**
- What will you say? This is called your **content.**
- How will you say it? This is called your **voice.**
- Who will read it? This is called your **audience.**

Sometimes, however, you are writing for a test. Then some of these things are already decided for you. Here is a question from a test.

> Many <u>popular board games, such as checkers,</u> can also be played on the <u>computer.</u> Write an article for students in a <u>game club</u> about how board games and computer games are <u>alike</u> and how they are <u>different.</u> In your article, be sure to include:
> - how board games and computer board games are alike
> - how they are different

The question tells you the purpose is to show how two things are the same and how they are different. It also tells you the subject is board games and the audience is students in a game club. The rest is up to you. You need to think about what you will write. Many writers begin by underlining important words. Look at the words underlined in the test question. Writers also make notes about what they will write.

Read
**Note**
Organize

Sometimes a graphic organizer can help you plan your writing. It can help you decide which ideas to use and their importance. For this assignment, you might use a Venn diagram like this one.

Read
Note
**Organize**

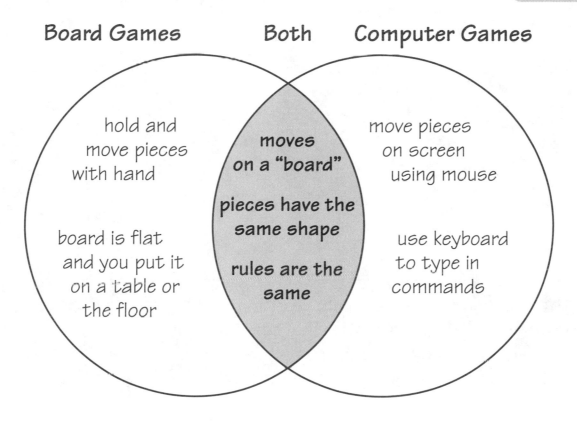

Board Games | Both | Computer Games

- hold and move pieces with hand
- board is flat and you put it on a table or the floor

**moves on a "board"**
**pieces have the same shape**
**rules are the same**

- move pieces on screen using mouse
- use keyboard to type in commands

There are other types of graphic organizers you can use for different types of writing. Here are some examples:

- **Cluster map or web**—This organizer works for many kinds of writing. It can help you to get your ideas on paper.
- **Sequence chart or story map**—A sequence chart is best when you are writing a narrative, or story. It helps you map out events in the order they happen.
- **Cause and effect chart**—This shows you the connection between what happened and the effect it had on other things.

# Guided Practice

Many people like to play sports. You can play sports as part of a team. Or, you can play sports individually. Swimming is an individual sport. Baseball is a team sport. Write an article for the school newspaper about how swimming and baseball are alike and how they are different. In your article, be sure to include:

- how swimming and baseball are alike
- how they are different

Who is the audience?

A  parents

B  teachers

C  sports fans

D  students

The question tells you to write an article for the school newspaper. You know that students in the school are the main people reading the newspaper. Choice D is the correct answer. Parents and teachers may read the newspaper. However, the newspaper is written for students. Choices A, B, and C are incorrect.

What type of organizer could you use to organize your writing?

**A** sequence chart

**B** idea web

**C** Venn diagram

**D** cause and effect chart

A sequence chart shows when things happened. An idea web helps you connect related ideas. A cause and effect chart shows what happened and why. Choices A, B, and D are incorrect. The correct answer is choice C. A Venn diagram is the best choice for comparing two things.

Which of these words would you underline to help understand the question?

**A** swimming

**B** sports

**C** team

**D** people

Choice A is the correct answer. The question asks you to compare swimming and baseball. Swimming is a key word. Choices B, C, and D are incorrect. These are not key words to help you understand the question.

## Step 2: Drafting

In the first step, you worked out your writing plan. Now, it is time to put your ideas into sentences and paragraphs. This step is called drafting. Don't worry about spelling and grammar yet. You can change things later. In this step, you just write down your ideas. You use the prewriting plan as a guide. Make sure each paragraph has a main idea. Then use details to support it. Use transition words and a concluding sentence. Here is a draft that could be written using the Venn diagram shown on page 7.

You can play many popular board games on a computer. The rules are the same. The game pieces look the same. But you play board games a little bit differently.

With a real board game, you have pieces and a board. you have to move the peices with your hand. The rules are on paper. You play with another person. I play Monopoly with my cousin.

A computr board game is played on a screen. You move the pieces with your mouse. The computer plays against you. You have to be smart to beat a Computer at checkers You can practice a lot.

Board games and computer board games are a lot alike. You learn how to play the same game in different ways. But it's on a screen, not a board.

## Step 3: Revising

You have finished drafting. The next step is revising. In this step, you read what you have written. Then you make changes to make your writing better. You edit your writing to make it clear. This way, your readers can easily understand your ideas.

When you revise, you can change your **content.** Or you might need to change your **structure.** Ask yourself these questions. Your answers will help you think about changes that will make your writing better.

## Content

- Does my writing have a main idea?
- Have I used enough details?
- Do I need to add important details? Where?
- Do I need to take out details that aren't important? Where?
- Does my writing have a beginning, a middle, and an end?

## Structure

- Is my writing organized in a way that fits the topic?
- Are my ideas clear?
- Do I need to make my ideas clearer?
- What words, phrases, or sentences should I add?
- Do my sentences say what I want them to say?
- Are my sentences well written?

# Guided Practice

**Read the revised draft. Look for changes. Then answer the questions.**

You can play many popular board games on a computer.

The rules are the same. The game pieces look the same. But

you play board games a little bit differently, **on a computer**

With a real board game, you have pieces and a board. you

have to move the peices with your hand. The rules are on

paper. **and** You play with another person. ~~I play Monopoly with~~

~~my cousin.~~

A computr board game is played on a screen. You move

the pieces with your mouse. **You can read the rules on the screen.** The computer plays against

you. You have to be smart to beat a Computer at checkers

You can practice a lot. **because computers never get tired of playing with you**

Board games and computer board games are a lot alike.

You learn how to play the same game in different ways.

**Both ways help you become a better player.**

~~But it's on a screen, not a board~~

Why did the writer take out a sentence in paragraph 2?

_____

_____

> ✓ Revising includes both adding and deleting sentences to make your meaning clearer. Every sentence should support the main idea with essential information. Here is a sample answer:

The sentence did not support the main idea.
It was not important.

Why did the writer change the last sentence of the article?

_____

_____

_____

> ✓ The last paragraph is the conclusion of an article or story. It should sum up what the important points are or relate to them in some way. It relates to points made in the introductory paragraph. Here is a sample answer:

The sentence is a better closing sentence. It sums up what the writer thinks about board games and computer board games.

What do you think would be a good title for this article?

_____

_____

✔ The title often sums up the main idea of an article or story. Here is a sample answer:

_A good title for this article is "Playing Board Games on a Computer."_

## Peer Review

The teacher might sometimes have students work in pairs to edit each other's papers. This is called **peer editing** or **peer review.** Students use a checklist, or **rubric,** to do this. The rubric explains what is needed to receive certain scores on a writing paper.

The rubric tells what is expected for a range of scores. Sometimes one rubric is used for the whole writing task. Other times two rubrics are used. One is for the content and how it is developed. The other is for grammar, punctuation, and capitalization. Rubrics for writing may differ but they should look something like the one on page 14.

# Checklist for Comparing and Contrasting

**Score 3**
- The writing answers all parts of the question.
- There are at least two clear similarities and two clear differences.
- The topic sentence clearly states the main idea.
- Important details are given in an order that makes sense.
- The writing is easy to read and stays on the subject.
- There are almost no mistakes in grammar, capitalization, punctuation, and spelling.

**Score 2**
- The writing answers almost all parts of the question.
- There are two generally clear similarities and two generally clear differences.
- The topic sentence could state the main idea more clearly.
- Some important details are not in order.
- The writing mostly sticks to the subject.
- There are some mistakes in grammar, capitalization, punctuation, and spelling.

**Score 1**
- The writing answers only part of the question.
- There are not two clear differences or two clear similarities.
- There is no topic sentence.
- Many important details are not in order.
- The writing is off the subject in many places.
- There are several mistakes in grammar, capitalization, punctuation, and spelling.

# Step 4: Editing

You have revised your work. Once you are happy with it, you can do the next step. You can edit your work. That means you read what you have written. You check to be sure everything is right. You look for grammar mistakes. You also look for mistakes in spelling, capitalization, and punctuation. You edit to make sure that:

- subjects and verbs agree
- the pronoun forms are right
- all words are spelled correctly
- proper nouns are capitalized

When you edit, you go over each sentence. You look for mistakes to be changed. This is called proofreading. When you proofread, you use marks to show changes. The chart below shows you some marks to use.

## Proofreading Symbols

| | |
|---|---|
| ∧ Add letters or words. | This game is played ∧ a computer. (on) |
| ⊙ Add a period. | These cards are for the board game⊙ |
| ≡ Capitalize a letter. | ≡you can practice a lot. |
| ⌃ Add a comma. | We brought the game, some food⌃and balloons. |
| ⌐ Take out letters or words. | You have the ~~board and~~ game. |
| ∿ Switch the position of letters or words. | Use the (red large) pieces. |

# Guided Practice

**Practice using proofreading marks with this paragraph.**

You can many popular board games on a
computer. the rules are the same The game pieces
look the same. But you play board games a little
bit differently a on computer.

> ✓ Were you able to find all the mistakes? Here are the corrections:
> Sentence 1: insert *play* between the words *can* and *many*
> Sentence 2: capitalize the word *the* and insert a period after the word *same*
> Sentence 4: switch the prepositions *a* and *on*

Look at the draft below with its proofreading corrections. Can you identify them? You should find six proofreading corrections. Circle them on the draft.

_____

**(write your article title above)**

You can play many popular board games on a computer.

The rules are the same. The game pieces look the same. But

you play board games a little bit differently. on a computer

With a real board game, you have pieces and a board. you

have to move the pieces with your hand. The rules are on

paper. You play with another person. I play Monopoly with

my cousin.

A computer board game is played on a screen. You move
the pieces with your mouse. **You can read the rules on the screen.** The computer plays against
you. You have to be smart to beat a Computer at checkers. **because computers never get tired of playing with you.**
You can practice a lot.

Board games and computer board games are a lot alike.

You learn how to play the same game in different ways.
**Both ways help you become a better player.**
~~But it's on a screen, not a board.~~

✔ Did you find all the corrections? Here are the correct answers:

Sentence 6: circle you. This should be capitalized, You.
    Circle peices. The word is misspelled. It should be pieces.
Sentence 7: circle you. This should be lowercase, you.
Sentence 8: circle computr. The word is misspelled. It
    should be computer.
Sentence 12: circle Computer. This should be lowercase:
    computer.
    Circle checkers. There should be a period after this word.

# Step 5: Publishing

Once you have fixed any mistakes or problems with your
work, you are ready to publish it. Publishing means to share
your work with other people. This is the last stage of writing. You
might turn your paper into your teacher. Or, you may read it to
the class. Maybe, you are asked to create a poster or PowerPoint
presentation with your work. Publishing can take many forms.

# Test Yourself

Some children share a bedroom with a sister or brother. Others have a room of their own. Write two paragraphs that compare and contrast sharing a bedroom and having a bedroom to yourself. When writing your paragraphs, be sure to do the following:

- follow all the steps of the writing process
- tell how sharing or having your own bedroom are alike
- tell how sharing or having your own bedroom are different
- use details to support your ideas

**1** What are you being asked to write about?

_____

_____

_____

_____

_____

**Read**
Note
Organize

**2** Look for key words. Underline them. Write the key words below.

Read
**Note**
Organize

_____

_____

_____

_____

_____

**3** Use the Venn diagram to plan your writing.

Read
**Note**
**Organize**

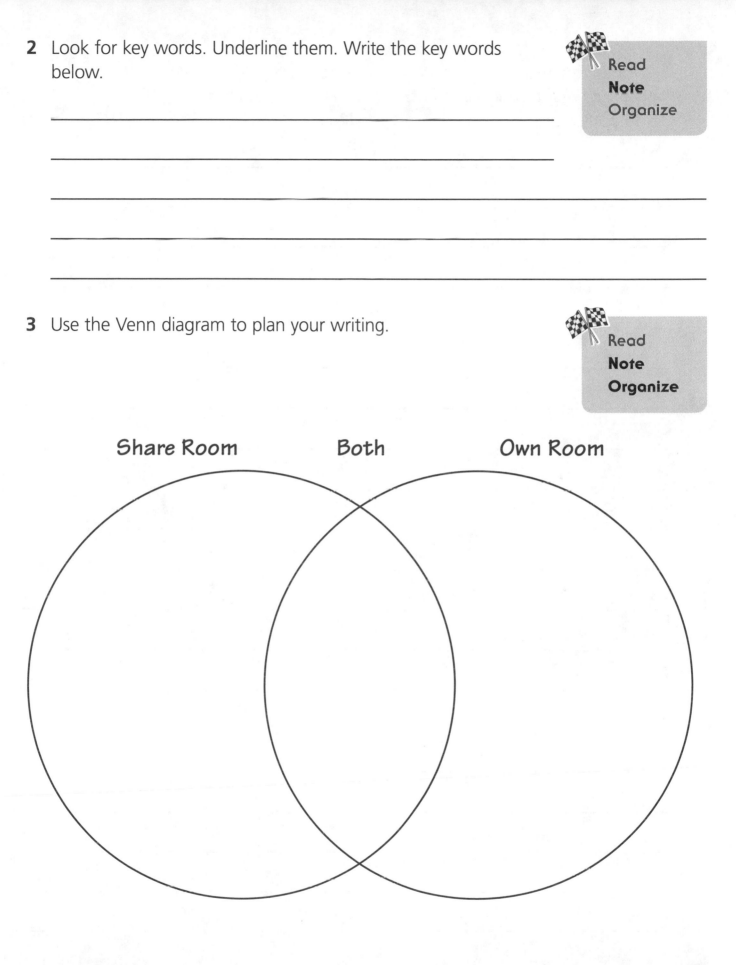

Share Room          Both          Own Room

**4** Write a rough draft of your topic. Your draft should show how sharing a room or having your own room are the same and how they are different. Use details to make your paragraphs clear.

_____

_____

_____

_____

_____

_____

_____

_____

_____

_____

_____

_____

_____

_____

_____

**UNIT 1** ❊❊❊❊❊❊❊❊❊❊❊❊❊❊❊❊❊❊❊❊❊❊❊❊❊❊❊❊❊❊❊❊❊❊❊❊
Elements of Writing

**5** You have written your draft. Now, read it again carefully. Change the content if you need to. Then edit your revision. Use the checklist or rubric on page 14 to review your writing.

_____

_____

_____

_____

_____

_____

_____

_____

_____

_____

_____

_____

_____

_____

_____

_____

**6** Then write your final answer on the lines below. Show your writing to your teacher. Or, exchange papers with another student. Review each other's writing. Give it a score using the rubric on page 14.

# Writing a Paragraph

W.3.4–6

The paragraph is the foundation for all the writing you do. A good paragraph has one main idea. All of the sentences in the paragraph should be about the main idea. The **topic sentence** tells the main idea of the paragraph. This sentence is usually the first sentence of the paragraph. The rest of the sentences give details or facts about the main idea. The last sentence is the concluding sentence. It sums up the paragraph. Or, it may help connect the paragraph to the other paragraphs that follow.

## Guided Practice

**Read the paragraphs. Then answer the questions.**

The Metropolitan Zoo is an exciting place to learn about animals. On your first visit, you may be surprised that many animals are not in cages. They have lots of space to run around and roam. At the Metropolitan Zoo, plants and trees are almost everywhere. The monkeys can climb, the birds can nest, and the lions have a shady place to sleep. The only place you won't find plants is in the penguin enclosure. There, penguins slip and slide around on the ice and swim in ocean water. The water is kept very cold, just the way they like it! When you visit the Metropolitan Zoo, you will have a good idea of how each animal lives in the wild.

What is the topic sentence in the paragraph?

**A** The Metropolitan Zoo is an exciting place to learn about animals.

**B** They have lots of space to run around and roam.

**C** The only place you won't find plants is in the penguin enclosure.

**D** When you visit the Metropolitan Zoo, you will have a good idea of how each animal lives in the wild.

First, look for the main idea. This will help you find the topic sentence in the paragraph. Choice A is the correct answer. The topic is the "Metropolitan Zoo." The topic sentence tells you that you are going to read about what you can learn at the zoo.

Topic: Collecting Rocks and Minerals

_____ You don't need to dig in a mine to be a rock collector! You can find some minerals just by searching in rock beds. Pyrite, or fool's gold, is a mineral that may be lying on the ground. You need a tool called a pick to find other minerals. A pick can break apart rocks and soil. Geodes look like plain rocks on the outside. But

when you break them apart, you might find a surprise inside! You might find amethyst, a mineral that is used in jewelry. Rock collecting is a fun hobby for anyone interested in nature and science.

Write a topic sentence for the paragraph.

_____

_____

> ✔ First, look at the topic. Then read the rest of the paragraph. Ask yourself: What is the main idea? Keep in mind that the topic sentence does not have to be the first sentence in the paragraph. Here is a sample answer:

*Have you ever thought about collecting rocks and minerals?*

## Organizing the Paragraph

A good paragraph makes sense. Every sentence should be about the topic. The sentences should also be in an order that makes sense. This flowchart shows the order of the sentences in the paragraph about the Metropolitan Zoo on page 23.

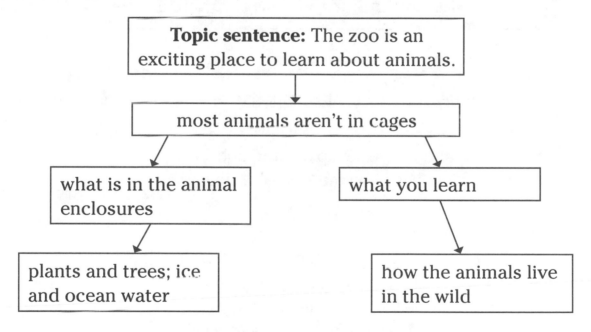

If you are writing just one paragraph, you should end with a closing sentence. The closing sentence of the paragraph on page 23 is, "When you visit the Metropolitan Zoo, you will have a good idea of how each animal lives in the wild." It finishes the paragraph and makes a statement about the topic.

# Guided Practice

You need to wear sturdy boots or shoes.

You should carry water, too.

Hiking is a great way to get exercise.

It's easy to start hiking.

_____

_____

_____

✓ The first step is to decide which sentence is the topic sentence. Next, number the sentences in the order you will use them. Then use this order to write the sentences in the form of a paragraph. Finally, write a closing sentence. Here is a sample answer:

> Hiking is a great way to get exercise. It's easy to start hiking. You need to wear sturdy boots or shoes. You should carry water, too. That way, you'll be able to enjoy hiking!

There is more than one way to set up a paragraph. Which order will you choose? It depends on the kind of writing you are doing.

Sometimes you are writing a paragraph to explain something. You can do this two ways. You can give **details** that support your main idea. This is what the paragraph about the Metropolitan Zoo on page 23 does. The other way is to give **examples** of the main idea. That is what the paragraph about rock collecting on page 24 does.

When you write a story, you should use **time order.** You need to tell the events in the order that they happened. Connecting words and phrases help you put events in time order. Use words such as *first, then, after that, later,* and *finally.*

If you are describing a scene, you should use **location.** Explain where things are in your description. If you want to describe a new park, you might use connecting words and phrases such as *close by, in the distance,* or *around.*

Sometimes you must write a short answer to a question on a test. These answers should be in the form of a paragraph. You have a limited amount of time to write your answer. However, if you use the same steps in the writing process, you should be able to finish in time. Use these steps to write your answer in the time you are given.

1. Underline the key words. This will help you understand the question.
2. Think about what you want to say.
3. Decide which plan you will use to set up your paragraph.
4. Write your topic sentence first. Then finish your paragraph.
5. Check your answer. You can still make changes before time is called.

## Guided Practice

**Read this passage about school lunches. Then answer the question.**

Many children eat school lunches. But do they know how the menus are put together? What goes into a good school lunch, anyway?

School lunches always have to have a main dish. This might be meatloaf, pizza, or fish fillets. Usually, a main dish has some protein. This can come from lean meat, fish, or cheese. Side dishes are usually vegetables. A healthy side dish might be a serving of salad, string beans, or corn. Don't skip those veggies!

Then comes dessert. Many schools try to give healthy choices for dessert. It's nice to have sweets, but a serving of fruit is better for you. Maybe an apple with that cookie might give you more energy! Make the right choices at lunch, and you'll be healthy for years to come.

> What do you eat for lunch at school? Do you eat in a cafeteria? Do you bring your lunch from home? Write a paragraph about a healthy school lunch that you like to eat. Be sure to include:
>
> • why it is a good choice for lunch
>
> • details and examples that support your choice

_____

_____

_____

_____

_____

Here is how one student, Jayden, wrote his answer. First, he underlined important parts of the question. Then he made some notes. He knew he would need to write a story about his own experience with choosing a school lunch. He decided to use details and examples to set up the events in his story.

**Read**
**Note**
Organize

To plan his writing, Jayden used a web. He wrote down the main idea in the middle of the web. Then he listed the details that he wanted to use in the outer circles.

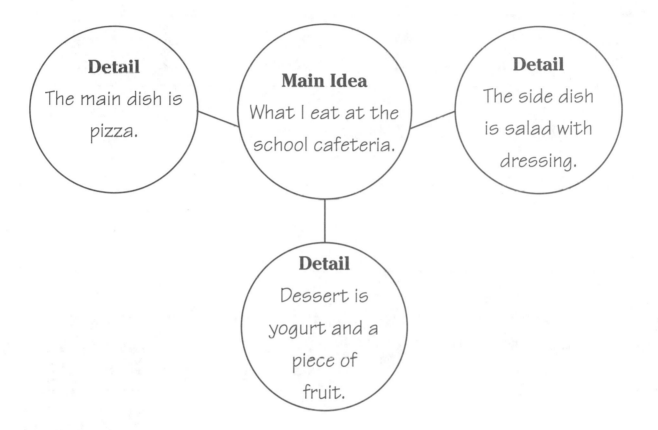

Then he used the details that he listed to write his paragraph.

✓ Jayden also used time sequence in his paragraph. Here is what he wrote:

I eat lunch at my school cafeteria. I try to pick healthy things to eat. The best meal is pizza. I always get a salad with it. I put some dressing on the salad. For dessert, I usually eat yogurt and a piece of fruit. There are apples and bananas. I like peaches the best, though. This is my favorite healthy lunch.

What is Jayden's topic sentence?

_____

_____

✓ What is the main idea of Jayden's paragraph? The topic sentence will tell you what the paragraph is about. Here is a sample answer:

_____I try to pick healthy things to eat._____

List a detail or example that Jayden used in his paragraph.

_____

_____

✓ The supporting sentences relate to the topic sentence. They give details that support this main idea. Or, they give examples. Here is a sample answer:

_____I always get a salad._____

What is his closing sentence?

_____

_____

✓ The closing sentence ends the paragraph by connecting back to the main idea. Here is a sample answer:

_____This is my favorite healthy lunch._____

# Test Yourself

## Answer the questions.

1  Which would make the *best* topic sentence of a paragraph about pirates?

   **A**  Pirates once sailed the seas in search of treasure.

   **B**  A few pirates were women.

   **C**  They took everything from food to gold.

   **D**  Pirates climbed aboard other ships to steal anything that was valuable.

2  Which would make the *best* topic sentence of a paragraph about marbles?

   **A**  Many children like to trade their marbles with each other.

   **B**  Marbles come in every color under the sun.

   **C**  Marbles are very popular in our school.

   **D**  Children have marble contests on the playground.

3  Which would make the *best* topic sentence of a paragraph about art classes?

   **A**  The most popular art class is origami.

   **B**  Some students take two or three different classes.

   **C**  You can take classes in any type of art you like.

   **D**  Our after-school program offers many art classes.

4  Which would make the *best* topic sentence of a paragraph about skating?

   **A**  Inline skating is a great way to get exercise if done safely.

   **B**  It takes a lot of practice at first.

   **C**  It is important to dress for safety when inline skating.

   **D**  You should wear a helmet, knee and elbow pads, and wrist guards.

**UNIT 1**
**Elements of Writing**

31

**5** Read the question. Then write your response.

> The passage on pages 27–28 ends with the sentence: "Make the right choices at lunch, and you'll be healthy for years to come." Explain what the writer means by this sentence. Write your answer in the form of a paragraph. Be sure to include:
> - a topic sentence that gives your main idea
> - details that back up your main idea

_____

_____

_____

_____

_____

_____

_____

_____

_____

_____

_____

_____

# Main Idea and Details

W.3.2, 4–6, 8, 9

The **main idea** is what the text is about. The details in the text support or explain the main idea. In Lesson 2, you learned about topic sentences. A **topic sentence** is the main idea of a paragraph.

## Guided Practice

**Read the passage. Then answer the question.**

Many boys and girls have some baseball cards. Lots of them love baseball, and they want to have cards of the players. Some children start a real collection. They try to get all the players on a team or all of their favorite players.

Baseball cards have been made since 1869. They were sold with products like gum and candy. During World War II, there was a paper shortage. Cards were not produced during the war. The Bowman Gum Company started to make the cards again in 1948. Then Topps began making them in 1951. That's when the collecting game took off. Children bought the cards by the hundreds! Even adults got in on the game a little bit.

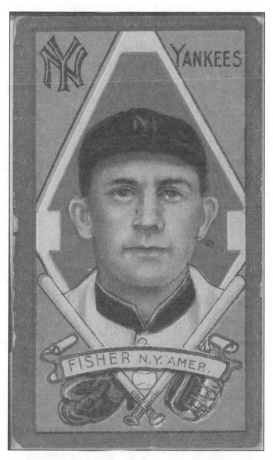

In 1980, more candy companies made the cards. Then adults started collecting them, too. Some of the older cards were worth thousands of dollars!

If you want to start collecting baseball cards, you can find them at hobby shops. You can also still buy them with gum. Once you start collecting, you get to the fun part. You can get good cards by trading with other collectors.

Collecting baseball cards used to be just for children. Now, it is a big hobby for both children and adults. Give it a try!

You have decided to start collecting baseball cards. Write a letter to a friend describing your new hobby. This letter should be one paragraph long.
Be sure to include:

• a topic sentence that states your main idea

• facts and details from the article that support the main idea

# Step 1: Prewriting

Here's how one student, Renee, answered the question. She knew she had to read the question more than once. Then she underlined the important words.

What key words do you think Renee underlined?

_____

_____

_____

✓ Looking for key words helps you know what to write about. You need to understand the purpose for writing and your audience. Here is a sample answer:

> Renee underlined <u>letter</u>, <u>paragraph</u>, <u>main idea</u>, and <u>facts and details</u>. This tells her she is writing a letter. The letter is only one paragraph. She needs to include facts and details that support the main idea.

Then Renee read the article again. This time she took notes to help her with her letter. Here are her notes:

topic—baseball card collecting
I will write for my friends
baseball cards have been around for more than 100 years
some cards are worth a lot of money
it used to be just for children
you can trade with other people
you can get cards at hobby shops

Renee's next step was to plan her writing. She used a web organizer to help her. She put her main idea in the center.

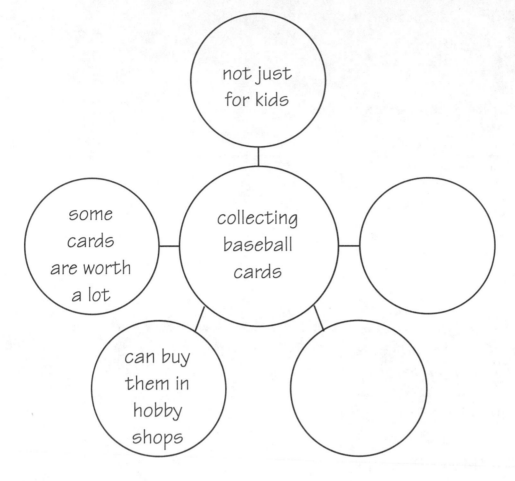

Which items below are details that fit in the chart? Put a check next to those that fit.

_____ You can trade with other people.

_____ People collect lots of things.

_____ My uncle played baseball as a child.

_____ Baseball cards have been around for more than 100 years.

✔ The details should support the main idea. The main idea is collecting baseball cards. Renee will only use details that support the main idea. Here are the details Renee used:

You can trade with other people.

Baseball cards have been around for more than 100 years.

Renee's next step is to write her draft.

# Step 2: Drafting

Dear Jennifer,

Guess what I am going to do. I'm going to start collecting baseball cards! They have been around for more than 100 years. Some really are valuable. I love baseball. I have some cards alredy. so I decide to collect them. You can buy the baseball cards in hobby shops. You can buy them in toy stores. It's not just for children. everyone collects them! Some people even trade the cards so I find some collectors to trade. Maybe if you start collecting baseball cards, we can trade to!

Love,

Renee

What is Renee's topic sentence?

_____

_____

✔ The main idea of the paragraph is the topic sentence. Here is what Renee wrote:

I'm going to start collecting baseball cards!

What are some details Renee gives to support the main idea?

_____

_____

✔ The facts and details used in the paragraph must support the main idea. They should give the reader more information about baseball card collecting. Here is a sample answer:

Renee told how old baseball cards are. She said they were valuable. Adults and children collect them. Some people trade them.

Is there any information missing from this draft?

_____

_____

✔ Renee wrote down her ideas in her draft. Are her sentences and information complete? Or, will the reader be confused because the information is incomplete? Here is a sample answer:

Some words are missing in her sentences.

What does Renee need to do to change her draft?

_____

_____

✔ The main idea of a draft is to use your prewriting plan to write down sentences and paragraphs. Most writers make changes later because there may be mistakes in spelling or grammar. Or, the sentences' meaning may not be clear. Does Renee have any problems to be corrected? Here is as sample answer.

_Yes, she needs to correct misspelled words. She also needs to rewrite sentences._

The next step is for Renee to revise what she has written.

# Step 3: Revising

**Read the revised draft carefully. Then answer the questions.**

Dear Jennifer,

Guess what I'm going to do. I'm going to start collecting baseball cards! They have been around for more than 100 years. Some ⌐really are⌐ valuable. ~~Hove baseball~~ I have some cards alredy, so I decide^d to collect them. You can buy the baseball cards in hobby shops. ~~You can buy them~~ ^and in toy stores, ~~It's~~ ^They're not just for kids. everyone collects them! Some people even trade the cards so I find some collectors ~~to~~ ^and ^with them trade. Maybe if you start collecting baseball cards, we can trade to!

Love,

Renee

Which two words did Renee switch?

_____

_____

✓ Sometimes a word might be in the wrong place in a sentence. Or, sometimes the sentence reads better when words are changed. Here is a sample answer:

Renee switched the order of really are to are really.

Which sentences did she combine? Write the new sentence.

_____

_____

✓ Writers often combine two sentences to avoid repeating information and because the information is connected in some way. Here is a sample answer:

Renee combined sentence 6 and sentence 7. The new sentence is: "You can buy the baseball cards in hobby shops and in toy stores."

# Peer Review

Renee might exchange papers with another student. They would review each other's work. Then they would give it a score based on the rubric. They would discuss ways to improve their work.

## Checklist for Writing Main Idea and Details

**Score 3**
- The writing answers all parts of the question.
- There is a clear main idea.
- The writing includes important details that support the main idea.
- The writing is easy to read and stays on the subject.
- Words are used correctly and well.
- There are almost no mistakes in grammar, capitalization, punctuation, and spelling.

**Score 2**
- The writing answers almost all parts of the question.
- There is a main idea, but it could be stated more clearly.
- Most details support the main idea.
- The writing mostly sticks to the topic, but there are some details that don't belong.
- Some words are not used correctly.
- There are some mistakes in grammar, capitalization, punctuation, and spelling.

**Score 1**
- The writing answers only part of the question.
- The writing does not include a clear main idea.
- Many details are missing or hard to understand.
- The writing is not easy to read and is off the subject in many places.
- Many words are overused or not used correctly.
- There are several mistakes in grammar, capitalization, punctuation, and spelling.

# Step 4: Editing

**Edit the draft for four more mistakes.**

_____

_____

_____

✓ Look for misspelled words and misplaced punctuation. Did you find all the mistakes? Here is a sample answer:

Sentence 1: Change the period after the word *do* to a question mark

Sentence 5: Change the spelling of the word *alredy* to *already*

Sentence 8: Capitalize the word *everyone*

Sentence 10: Change the word *to.* It should be *too.*

# Step 5: Publishing

The final step is for Renee to show her work to someone. She can do this by turning her paper into her teacher.

# Test Yourself

## Questions and Answers About Baseball Cards

**Q  When were baseball cards first made?**

**A**  In 1869; they didn't hit big production until after World War II. In 1980, when more candy companies got into card production, the hobby became very popular.

**Q  Are baseball cards worth a lot?**

**A**  Some older cards are very valuable. Some of these are also rare; only a few of them were made. Cards of star players are also worth more money. But you don't have to have a lot of money to collect baseball cards. Many card sets are priced low.

**Q  Where can I get baseball cards?**

**A**  You can get baseball cards at candy stores. You can also get them at hobby or toy stores. But the best way to get better cards is by trading. Find other people who love baseball cards, and see if they have something you want. Make a trade, talk about your cards, and have fun!

**Q  How do I keep my cards looking nice?**

**A**  Most collectors keep their cards in plastic card sleeves. You can get plastic cases to store each card. Or you can put the cards in binders. Either way, you should protect your cards. They will become more valuable over time. Keep them away from light, heat, and water. Your collection will last a lifetime!

You have decided to start a baseball card collecting club. Write an article for your student newsletter. Write about baseball card collecting, and why you want to start the club.

Be sure to include:

- a topic sentence that states your main idea
- a reason for starting the club
- important details about collecting baseball cards

**1** What kind of writing are you being asked to do?

**Read**
Note
Organize

_____

_____

_____

_____

**2** What will the structure of your writing look like?

Read
Note
**Organize**

_____

_____

_____

_____

_____

**3** Who will read your writing?

_____

_____

**4** One way to plan your writing might be to use a web to list details about the hobby. You can also create a chart to list your reasons for starting a club. Use a separate piece of paper for the chart.

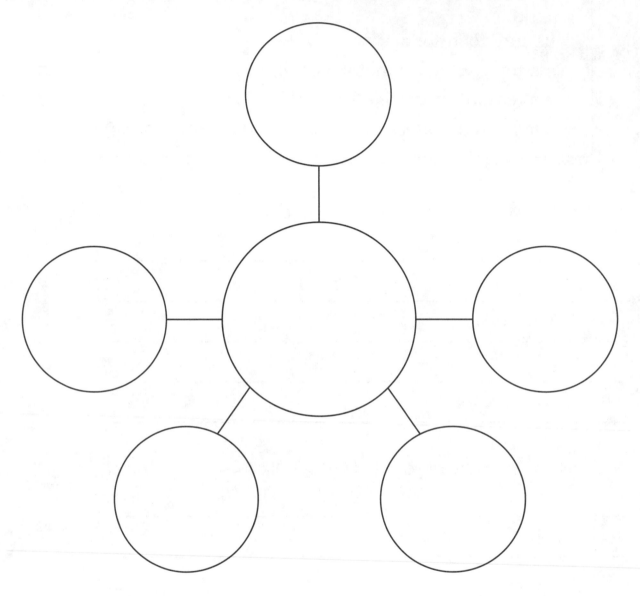

**5** Before you write your draft, look at your plan. Think about what your topic sentence should be. What do you need to explain in this article? Are your ideas in the correct order? Do you need to add details to make it clearer?

_____

_____

_____

_____

_____

_____

_____

_____

_____

_____

_____

_____

_____

_____

_____

_____

**6** When you have finished your draft, go back over it. Make your revisions on this page. Then proofread your draft for mistakes. Use the rubric or checklist on page 42 to review your own writing. Have a peer edit it if appropriate.

_____

_____

_____

_____

_____

_____

_____

_____

_____

_____

_____

_____

_____

_____

_____

_____

_____

**7** When you are satisfied with your writing, you are ready to
publish your work. Write your final copy on the lines below.
Then publish your work by showing it to your teacher

_____

_____

_____

_____

_____

_____

_____

_____

_____

_____

_____

_____

_____

_____

_____

# Cause and Effect

**W.3.2, 4–6, 8, 9**

When you read, you probably see connections between ideas and events. These connections explain why things happen. Your reading makes more sense when you understand these *why* connections. Look for clue words that signal **causes** *(because, since, due to)* and **effects** *(then, so, as a result)*.

## Guided Practice

**Read the passage. Then answer the question.**

### Beavers in the Neighborhood

A stream flows through a small town. Along the banks, trees are disappearing. Only pointed stumps remain. A nearby road is flooded. People in the neighborhood complain that their yards are soggy. Water is seeping into their basements. Why are these things happening?

Beavers have come to town. The beaver is an animal that lives in water. It cuts down trees with its sharp teeth. It eats parts of the tree and uses the rest for building. It uses branches, logs, mud, and plants to build a family home, called a lodge. It uses the same materials to build a dam. The dam holds back water so that the beavers have a pond to live in.

Beavers bring big changes to an area. The water behind their dams spreads out to create wetlands. Fish, turtles, frogs, and birds move into the wetlands. Scientists point out that wetlands provide homes for all kinds of living things. Wetlands are also valuable because they act like a filter that cleans water.

Other builders may be in the area, though—people! When people build homes in the same area that beavers use, the neighborhood may become more watery than people like. What is the result? In some places, laws allow the trapping of beavers. The troublesome beavers are removed. In other places, people protect the beavers' wetlands and find ways to control flooding. They learn to live with beavers in the neighborhood.

> The article "Beavers in the Neighborhood" tells about things that happen when beavers move into an area. Write a paragraph to explain three big changes that happen as a result of beavers' arrival. Use details from the article.
> In your paragraph, be sure to include:
> - the main cause of the changes
> - three big effects, or results
> - words that signal cause and effect connections, such as *because, reason, result,* and *so*

## Step 1: Prewriting

Here is how a student, Jamil, answered the test question. He created a plan to write his answer.

First, he read the question carefully. He underlined parts of the question to help him decide what to write.

He knows what kind of writing is expected. Jamil also knows how many details to include. He also understands that he needs to use signal words.

**Read**
Note
Organize

What words do you think Jamil underlined?

_____

_____

_____

✓ Jamil needs to know what kind of writing is expected. He should note any special words to be included. The number of details to be included is also important. Here is a sample answer:

Jamil underlined paragraph to explain three big changes, main cause, and three big effects. He also underlined words that signal cause and effect connections.

The next step after reading the question is to recognize cause and effect relationship. Jamil made a plan to show the ideas he would include in his paragraph. He decided to use a graphic organizer.

Read
Note
**Organize**

**EFFECT**
Roads, yards, and basements are watery.

**CAUSE**
Beavers cut down trees and build a dam.

**EFFECT**
Wetlands are created.

**EFFECT**
People decide whether to remove the beavers or protect the wetlands.

Jamil finished his chart. Then he wrote his topic sentence.

_The whole neighborhood changes when beavers move in._

He looked over his graphic organizer and decided to add details to his second effect.

_Wetlands are created._

Look back at the passage. What details from the passage do you think he added?

_____

_____

_____

_____

✓ An effect is what happens. Paragraph 3 gives information about what happens after a wetland is created. Here is a sample answer:

_Many kinds of wildlife like to live in wetlands._
_The wildlife may be fish, turtles, frogs, and birds._
_Wetlands are valuable because they act like a filter that_
_cleans water._

# Step 2: Drafting

A neighborhood can change when beavers move in. Beavers cut down trees to build a dam. The water that is held back by the dam makes a pond for them to live in. The water behind the dam can back up. The water spreads over the ground and gets in people's yard and basements. Sometimes, people trap the beavers and move them away so it wont build a dam. other people say that the beavers' dams create wetlands that are good for the water. These people think the beavers should be left alone because they make wetlands that should be protected.

What is Jamil's topic sentence?

**A** A neighborhood can change when beavers move in.

**B** Beavers cut down trees to build a dam.

**C** The water behind the dam can back up.

**D** The water that is held back by the dam makes a pond for them to live in.

> The topic sentence is the main idea. The other sentences support this main idea. Choices B, C, and D are details that support the main idea. Choice A is the correct answer.

Which of the following words did Jamil use to show cause and effect?

**A** when

**B** and

**C** that

**D** should

✓ Certain words show a connection between cause and effect. Choices B, C, and D do not show this connection. The correct answer is choice A. Other words that Jamil used to show this connection are *because* and *so.*

## Step 3: Revising

**Read Jamil's revised draft. Then answer the questions.**

A neighborhood can change when beavers move in.

Beavers cut down trees to build a dam. The water that is

held back by the dam makes a pond for them to live in.

The water behind the dam can back up. ~~The water~~ It spreads

over the ground and gets in people's yard and basements.

Sometimes, people trap the beavers and move them away

so it won't build a dam. other people say that the beavers'

dams create wetlands that provide homes for fish, frogs, and other animals. ~~are good for the water~~ These

people think the beavers should be left alone because they

make wetlands that should be protected.

Why did Jamil change the sentence "Other people say that the beavers' dams create wetlands that are good for the water."?

_____

_____

✓ Look at the changes Jamil made? Did they add information? Did they make the sentence clearer? These are some reasons that writers revise their sentences. Here is a sample answer:

_____Jamil changed the sentence to give reasons why the_____
wetlands are good._____

Why did Jamil change "The water" to "It" in sentence 5?

_____

_____

✓ Writers pay attention to the words they use and how they are used. They try to make each sentence different. Here is a sample answer:

Jamil used the word water in the sentence before this
one. He did not want to begin the sentence the same way.
So Jamil used a pronoun instead.

# Peer Review

Jamil used a rubric or checklist to review his writing. Then he traded papers with another student. They gave each other a score based on the rubric. Then they talked about ways to make their writing better.

## Checklist for Writing Cause and Effect

**Score 3**
- The writing answers all parts of the question.
- The writing clearly shows one cause and three effects.
- A topic sentence introduces the ideas in the paragraph.
- Words that signal causes and effects are used to point out connections.
- The writing is easy to read and stays on the subject.
- Capitalization and punctuation are correct.

**Score 2**
- The writing answers almost all parts of the question.
- The writing shows one cause and two effects.
- The topic sentence does not lead well into the paragraph.
- One word signals a cause and effect connection.
- The writing is fairly easy to read and mostly stays on the subject.
- There are some mistakes in capitalization and punctuation.

**Score 1**
- The writing answers only part of the question.
- The writing does not show the cause and any effects.
- There is no topic sentence.
- There are no words signaling a cause and effect connection.
- It is hard to tell what the subject is.
- There are many mistakes in capitalization and punctuation.

# Step 4: Editing

_____

_____

_____

✓ When you edit, look for words that are misspelled. Also, make sure that the writer used the correct punctuation and capitalization. Here is a sample answer:

Add an *s* to the word *yard* in sentence 5.

Change the word *it* to *they* in sentence 6.

Capitalize the word *other* in sentence 7.

# Step 5: Publishing

Jamil is ready for the next step. He is satisfied with this work. Now, he is ready to publish it. Instead of handwriting his essay, he will use a computer. Then he will turn it into the teacher.

Which of the following is another way for Jamil to publish his paper?

**A** record it

**B** make a PowerPoint presentation

**C** send it into the newspaper

**D** have a friend read it

✓ Think about why something was written. In this case, Jamil is doing an assignment for a class. Choices A, C, and D are ways to publish something. However, they are not the best way to publish a class assignment. Choice B is the correct answer. He could use pictures of wetlands and his essay to create a PowerPoint presentation.

# Town of Mairston Turns Off Screens

**April 29**—Television, computer, and game screens in Mairston have been dark for seven days. Why? Thousands of families in town chose to join the yearly event called Screen-Free Week. They wanted to see how interesting life would be without electronic media.

"I was bored at first," said 9-year-old Lena Bonds. "But by the end of the week, I didn't miss my shows at all. I played outside more, and I read three books."

At Mairston Public Library, "Children took out more books and board games than ever before," said librarian Ella Thomas. "Our evening story hour was so crowded, we had to split it into two sessions."

Screen-Free Week used to be called TV-Turnoff Week. The TV-Turnoff Network created TV-Turnoff Week in 1995. The group says that an American child spends 900 hours in school every year but watches more than 1,000 hours of television. This number rises if electronic media is included. That's just too much screen time, according to experts in education and health. The group wants children and adults to turn off all electronic media for a week.

When they stop watching television, using the computer, and playing electronic games, parents and children spend more time together, which strengthens family connections. Children read more, which leads to success in school. They play chess, make-believe, and other games that build their brain power. When the television is turned off, people become more active. They walk, run, hike, ride bikes, and play sports. Instead of sitting and using almost no energy, they get healthy exercise.

"We plan to cut back on screen time every week," said Lena's dad. "Screen-Free Week has shown us how many other things we can do instead."

> The article "Town of Mairston Turns Off Screens" tells about an event called Screen-Free Week. Write a paragraph to explain the results of turning off electronic media. Use details from the article.
> In your paragraph, be sure to include:
> - the reason for Screen-Free Week
> - three effects, or results, of turning televisions off
> - words that signal cause and effect connections, such as *reason, because, result,* and *so*

**1** What kind of writing are you being asked to do?

_____

_____

_____

_____

_____

Read
Note
Organize

**2** How many effects will you write about?

_____

_____

_____

_____

**3** Would you choose the word *because* to point out a cause or an effect?

_____

_____

_____

_____

**4** Use the cause and effect chart to plan your writing.

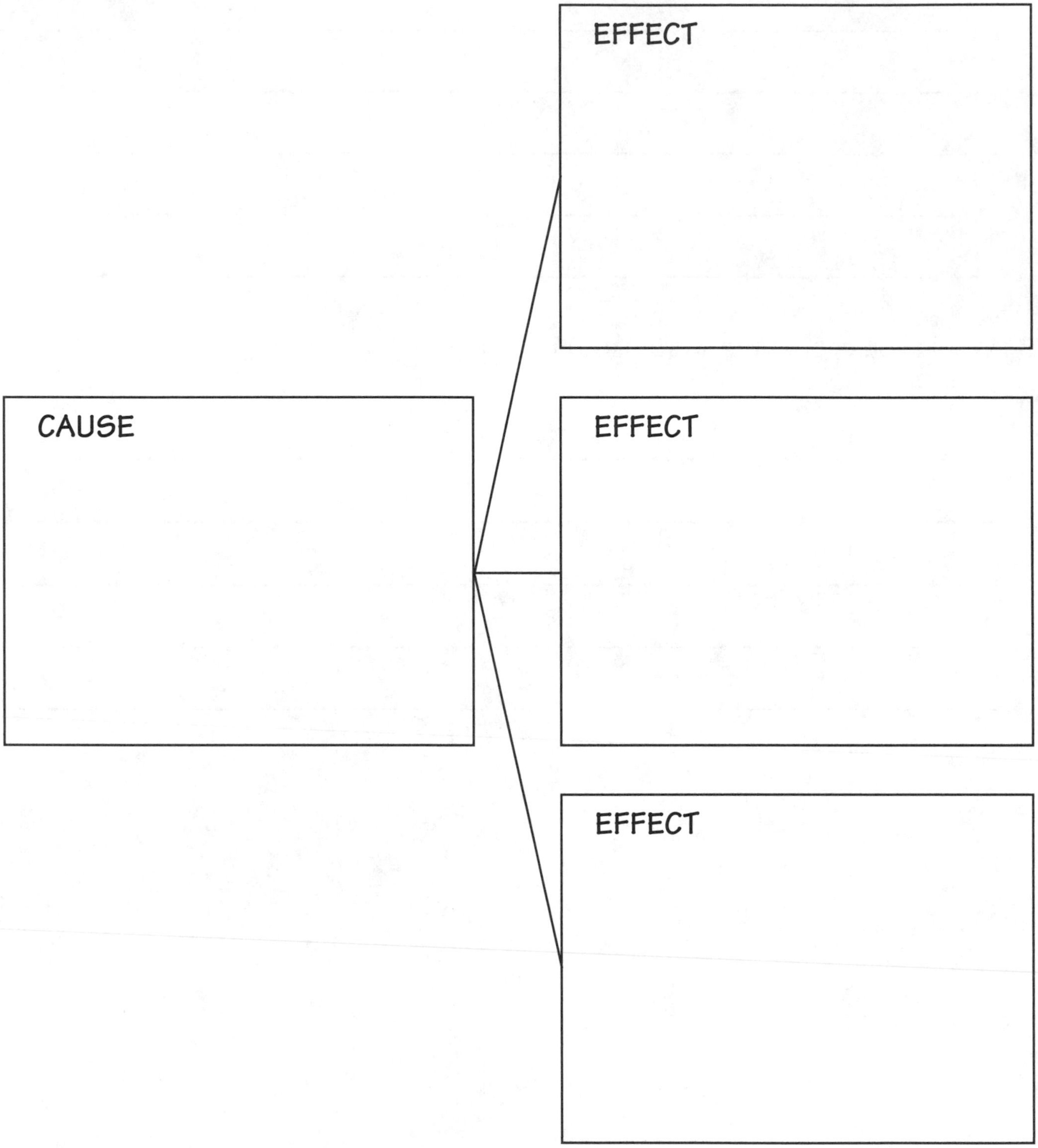

EFFECT

CAUSE

EFFECT

EFFECT

**5** Write your draft on the lines below. Use the cause and effect chart to help you write your draft. Remember to include the required information and special words that signal cause and effect connections.

_____

_____

_____

_____

_____

_____

_____

_____

_____

_____

_____

_____

_____

_____

**UNIT 1**
**Elements of Writing**
**63**

**6** When you have finished your draft, read it carefully. Revise it on this page. Use the rubric on page 57 to review your writing. Have a peer edit your writing if appropriate.

_____

_____

_____

_____

_____

_____

_____

_____

_____

_____

_____

_____

_____

_____

_____

**7** When you are satisfied with your writing, you are ready to publish your work. Write your final copy on the lines below. Publish your work by showing it to your teacher.

_____

_____

_____

_____

_____

_____

_____

_____

_____

_____

_____

_____

_____

_____

# Comparing and Contrasting

W.3.1, 2, 4–6, 8, 9

Some writing you do may ask you to explain how two things are the same. This is called **comparing.** You may also be asked to tell how two things are different. This is called **contrasting.**

## Guided Practice

**Read the passage. Then answer the questions.**

## A Tale of Two Brothers
### CHARLESTON, S.C.

The Charleston Historical Society plans to put on a new play about the Civil War. The play is titled "A Tale of Two Brothers." It tells about two brothers who fought against each other in the Civil War.

James and William Underhill grew up on a farm in Ohio. James loved to farm. He decided to stay in Ohio to work on the family farm. He raised chickens and cows. He also grew corn and wheat. William loved to read books, and he also enjoyed math. He wanted to live and work in a city, so he moved to Charleston, South Carolina. William worked as a clerk and joined a militia company. He loved everything about soldiers and weapons.

In Ohio, the call went out. Soldiers were needed to join the Union Army. James Underhill answered the call. He knew nothing about how to fight. But he knew that it was his duty to fight. In Charleston, the Confederate forces also put out the call. And William Underhill was one of the first men to sign up. He knew a lot about guns and cannons. He felt the call of duty, too. William wrote a letter to his brother. He told James where he would be fighting. James wrote back. It turned out that they would fight in the same battle.

This play tells the story of James and William Underhill. It is based on letters they wrote to each other. The story is not just a tale of the Civil War. It is a tale about the hardest battle of all—brother against brother.

> Stories are interesting when two characters are alike in some ways and different in other ways. Write two paragraphs that compare and contrast James and William Underhill in "A Tale of Two Brothers."
>
> In your answer, make sure that you use details from the story. Use details that show:
> - ways the two characters are the same
> - ways the two characters are different

## Step 1: Prewriting

One boy, Sam, was asked to write about these two brothers. First, he read the question. Then he underlined important information. He wanted to know who and what he was to write about.

**Read**
Note
Organize

What do you think Sam underlined?

_____

_____

_____

✓ Sam wants to know who he is writing about. He also wants to know what he is writing. Here's a sample answer:

Sam underlined this information: Write two paragraphs, James and William Underhill, ways that the two characters are the same, ways that the two characters are different.

The question does not say who the audience is. Sometimes it does say. It might be for other students or for a newspaper. Sam thinks that he knows the answer.

Which of the following is *most likely* the audience?

**A**   the teacher

**B**   the principal

**C**   a newspaper editor

**D**   Sam's parents

✓ Most of the writing that Sam does is in the classroom. His teacher is the person who usually gives him a writing topic. Choice A is the most likely answer. Choices B, C, and D are incorrect. If you do not know the audience, then write for the person who gave you the assignment. This is most often a teacher.

Sam's next step is to organize his ideas. He wants to use a graphic organizer to do this.

Read
Note
**Organize**

Which graphic organizer would help Sam the most?

**A**   web

**B**   sequence chart

**C**   cause and effect chart

**D**   Venn diagram

✓ Sam wants to give details about how the men are the same and how they are different. A web is helpful when organizing ideas that do not need to be in a certain order. A sequence chart helps show the order of events. The cause and effect chart shows what happened and why. Choices A, B, and C are incorrect. The correct answer is choice D.

Sam reread the passage. Then he filled in his graphic organizer.

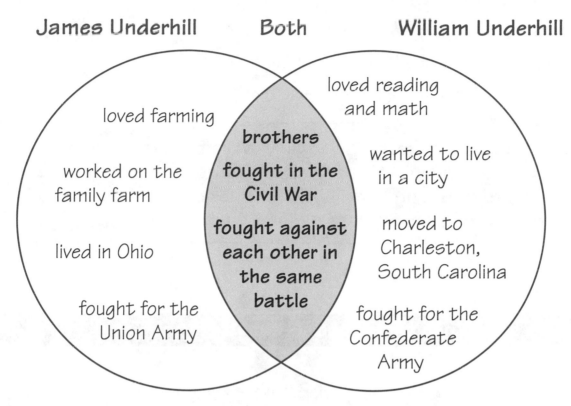

**James Underhill**

loved farming

worked on the family farm

lived in Ohio

fought for the Union Army

**Both**

brothers

**fought in the Civil War**

**fought against each other in the same battle**

**William Underhill**

loved reading and math

wanted to live in a city

moved to Charleston, South Carolina

fought for the Confederate Army

The next step is to structure his writing. There are different ways to organize a compare and contrast essay. Sam could discuss how the men are alike. Then he could discuss how they are different. Or, he could focus on one detail at a time and explain how each one is different and how each one is the same for the two men. Sam decided to explain how they are alike in paragraph 1. Then he would explain how they are different in paragraph 2.

Which of these details tells how the men are alike?

**A** The brothers fought in the Civil War.

**B** James wanted to be a farmer.

**C** William was a clerk.

**D** James lived in Ohio.

> Choices B, C, and D tell about only one brother. The correct answer is choice A. This tells how the brothers are alike.

Which of these details tells how the men are different?

**A** James and William were brothers.

**B** James and William grew up on a farm in Ohio.

**C** William moved to Charleston, South Carolina.

**D** James and William fought in the same battle.

 Choice C is the correct answer. Only William moved away from his home in Ohio. This is the only choice that tells how the brothers are different. Choices A, B, and D are incorrect. They tell how the brothers are alike.

## Step 2: Drafting

**Read Sam's draft. Then answer the questions.**

James and William Underhill were the same in some ways. They were brothers. They grew up on a farm. It was in Oho. James liked to be on the farm. They both fought in the Civil War, and they had to fight each other in a batle.

James and William were also different in many ways. James wanted to be a farmer. James stayed on the farm. He wanted to move to the city. He liked to read and liked math. he became a clerk. William knew a lot about weapons. He joined the army. James joined the army too. But because he had to. This is how the two brother ended up on different sides in the war.

What is Sam's topic sentence in paragraph 1?

 **A**  James and William were the same in some ways.

 **B**  They were brothers.

 **C**  They grew up on a farm.

 **D**  James and William were also different in many ways.

> Choices B and C are details. They support the main idea that the brothers are the same. Choice D is the topic sentence of paragraph 2. Choices B, C, and D are incorrect. The correct answer is choice A. This is the topic sentence of paragraph 1.

Which connecting word from Sam's draft does *not* signal a comparison?

 **A**  same

 **B**  and

 **C**  both

 **D**  different

> Sam used all these connecting words in his draft. Choices A, B, and C tell how the men are the same. These are incorrect. Only choice D signals a difference between the two men. See if you can find the connecting words in the draft.

Sam's next step is to revise his draft.

# Step 3: Revising

**Read the revised draft. Then answer the questions.**

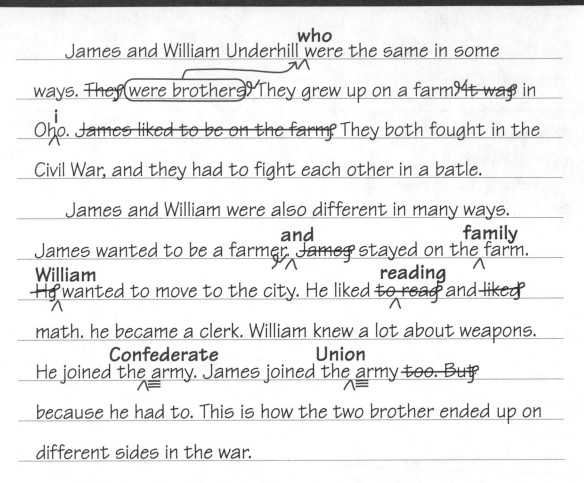

James and William Underhill who were the same in some

ways. ~~They~~ were brothers. They grew up on a farm. ~~It was~~ in

Ohio. ~~James liked to be on the farm.~~ They both fought in the

Civil War, and they had to fight each other in a batle.

James and William were also different in many ways.

James wanted to be a farmer. and ~~James~~ stayed on the farm.

William ~~He~~ wanted to move to the city. He liked ~~to read~~ reading and ~~liked~~

math. he became a clerk. William knew a lot about weapons.

He joined the Confederate army. James joined the Union army ~~too. But~~

because he had to. This is how the two brother ended up on

different sides in the war.

What sentence did Sam take out in paragraph 1?

**A** James and William Underhill were the same in some ways.

**B** They were brothers.

**C** They grew up on a farm.

**D** James liked to be on the farm.

✓ Sam used the delete sign to remove a sentence from paragraph 1. Choices A, B, and C had changes. However, they were not taken out of the paragraph. Choice D is the correct answer.

Why did Sam take the sentence out of paragraph 1?

_____

_____

_____

✓ The supporting sentences should add details or examples that support the main idea. Here is a sample answer:

Sam took the sentence out because it was not important to the topic. The topic is how the two brothers are alike. This sentence explains how James felt about the farm.

Why did Sam add the names of the armies in paragraph 2?

_____

_____

✓ Sometimes the writer adds information to make a sentence clearer. Or, the writer adds information that is important to the main idea. Here's a sample answer:

Sam added the names of the armies to make it clear that the brothers fought in different armies.

# Peer Review

Sam used the rubric to review his writing. Then he exchanged papers with another student. They reviewed each other's writing and gave it a score based on the rubric. Then they discussed ways they could each improve their writing.

## Checklist for Comparing and Contrasting

**Score 3**
- The writing answers all parts of the question.
- There are at least two clear similarities and two clear differences.
- The topic sentences clearly state the main idea of each paragraph.
- Important details are given in an order that makes sense.
- The writing is easy to read and stays on the subject.
- Capitalization and punctuation are correct.

**Score 2**
- The writing answers almost all parts of the question.
- There are two generally clear similarities and two generally clear differences.
- The topic sentences could state the main idea more clearly.
- Some important details are not in order.
- The writing mostly sticks to the subject.
- There are some mistakes in capitalization and punctuation.

**Score 1**
- The writing answers only part of the question.
- There are not two clear differences or two clear similarities.
- There are no topic sentences.
- Many important details are not in order.
- The writing is off the subject in many places.
- There are many mistakes in capitalization and punctuation.

# Step 4: Editing

_____

_____

_____

✓ When you edit, look for words that are misspelled. Also, make sure that the writer used the correct punctuation and capitalization. Here is a sample answer:

Change the word *batle* to *battle* in sentence 3.

Capitalize the word *he* in sentence 8.

Change the word *brother* to *brothers* in the last sentence.

# Step 5: Publishing

Sam published his paper by turning it into his teacher. He decided to handwrite it on another piece of paper rather than use the computer. Then he turned it in.

## Two Activities Added to the After-School Club

The After-School Club is adding two new activities to its list of fun things for kids to do after school. Come and join us!

The first new activity is hip-hop dancing. This activity will start in January. It will be taught by everyone's favorite gym teacher, Mr. Lopez. If you like hip-hop music and you like to jump around, this activity is for you! Bring comfortable clothes, like sweatpants and T-shirts. Be sure to wear sneakers, too. It's great exercise and lots of fun! This activity will take place in the north side of Rockwell Gym.

The other new activity also starts in January. Many kids have said they want to learn to play soccer. Well, now you can! The After-School Club's own Mrs. Anders will teach a soccer clinic. Mrs. Anders is a former women's soccer champion. She will show you all the right moves. Wear comfortable clothes like sweats and T-shirts, and don't forget your sneakers! This activity will be held in the south side of Rockwell Gym.

From music to sports, the After-School Club will have it all this January. Be active, have fun, and try something new at the After-School Club!

This article describes two new activities at the After-School Club. Write two paragraphs comparing and contrasting these activities. One paragraph should show how the activities are the same. One paragraph should show how they are different. Be sure to:

- tell at least two ways that they are the same
- tell at least two ways that they are different
- use details from the article to support your answer

1  What kind of writing are you being asked to do?

_____

_____

_____

_____

**Read**
Note
Organize

2  How will you structure your writing? (Two sentences? One paragraph? An interview?)

_____

_____

_____

_____

Read
Note
**Organize**

**3** To plan your essay, use the Venn diagram.

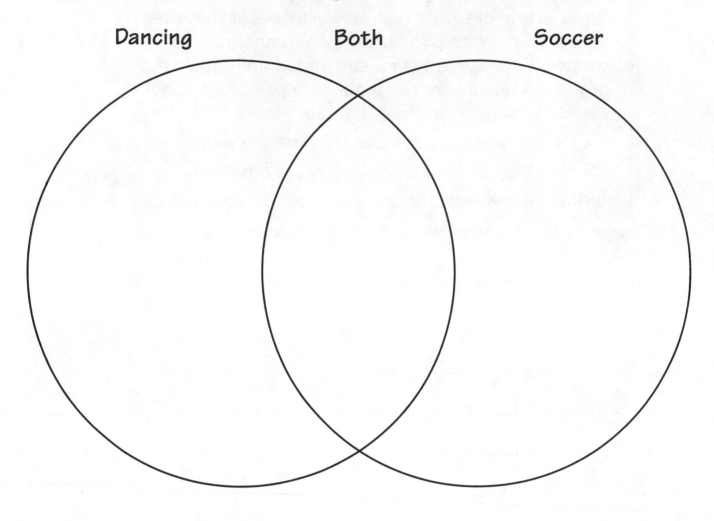

Dancing          Both          Soccer

List ideas from your Venn diagram that you will put in each paragraph.

Paragraph 1 _____

_____

_____

_____

Paragraph 2 _____

_____

_____

_____

**4** Now, you will write your own draft. Use your Venn diagram and paragraph plans to help write the draft. Be sure to use a topic sentence for each paragraph. In paragraph 1, write how the two activities are the same. In paragraph 2, write how they are different.

_____

_____

_____

_____

_____

_____

_____

_____

_____

_____

_____

_____

_____

_____

**5** When you have finished your draft, go back over it. Make your changes on this page. Check your draft for spelling, punctuation, and grammar mistakes. Use the rubric on page 74 to review your own writing. Ask a peer to edit it if appropriate.

**6** Then write your final answer below. Publish it by showing it to your teacher.

_____

_____

_____

_____

_____

_____

_____

_____

_____

_____

_____

_____

_____

_____

_____

_____

# Types of Writing

You use the same writing steps for all the writing that you do. You want to plan what you will write. Then you want to write it. Once you write it, you want to make sure it is correct. The final step is to publish it. The types of writing you do are different. You might write a story. Or, you might write to give someone information. Writing a story or narrative is different than writing for information. This unit will review the different types of writing.

- **In Lesson 6,** you will write an opinion. You will use facts in your writing, too. This will help support your opinion. It will also persuade someone to agree with you.

- **Lesson 7** is about descriptive writing. In this type of writing, you describe something. You create a word picture of the scene for your readers.

- **In Lesson 8,** you'll write a narrative. A narrative is a story with a beginning, middle, and end.

- **Lesson 9** tells how to write an informational text. This is the type of writing you do in class and on tests.

# Reasoned Writing

**W.3.1, 4, 5**

Some writing asks what you think or feel about something. This is called an **opinion.** You might be asked to persuade someone of your view. This is called persuasive writing, or reasoned writing. This type of writing uses **facts.** Facts can be proved. They can be checked.  You give reasons for your opinion in this type of writing. Then you use facts and examples to support your opinion. The last paragraph or statement sums up your opinion.

## Guided Practice

**Read the article. Then answer the questions.**

## How Should We Use Lakeside School's New Space?

Major changes are happening at Lakeside School. This year, classrooms were redone to make them brighter and more modern. Next year, a big, new space will be built next to the cafeteria. This space was supposed to be used for sports. However, many people spoke out against this idea. They pointed out that Lakeside School already has a gymnasium, but there is no good space for the arts.

Many students at Lakeside School are interested in the arts. They need a good place for art classes and activities. Other students are eager to start a theater club. They want a space where it would be easy to put on plays. These students are asking for a stage for plays and an area to try on and store costumes. There might even be room in the new space for dance classes. Right now, art classes are crowded into a small room, and the cafeteria is the only place to put on plays.

**UNIT 2** ▨▨▨▨▨▨▨▨▨▨▨▨▨▨▨▨▨▨▨▨▨▨▨▨▨▨▨▨▨▨
Types of Writing

Students who play sports want a new gymnasium. Some of them want to start soccer and basketball teams. New teams would need more space so that everyone could practice at the same

time. Students say that better space for sports activities would also encourage more kids to play sports.

Parents, too, have different opinions on this issue. Those with kids on sports teams want the space to be used as a gym. Parents of kids who want to start a theater club support an arts center. One thing is certain: Lakeside School is growing. Space is needed for many activities. Maybe sports and the arts will end up sharing the new space!

---

Does your school have a large gymnasium? Does it have space for art classes and for putting on plays? What if your school was getting a new, large space and students could help decide its use? Write an article for your school's newsletter stating whether you would use the space for sports or for the arts. Write two or more good reasons why you have this opinion.

---

## Step 1: Prewriting

Here is how one student, Mariah, answered the question. First, she read the question and underlined key words. She underlined *article, newsletter, sports or arts, opinion,* and *two reasons.*

Read
Note
Organize

Mariah also made notes while she read.

Read
**Note**
Organize

> my subject—a new space in my school
> what I have to write—a paragraph for my
> school newsletter
> who will read my writing—readers of the
> school newsletter
> what I have to do—write two or more good
> reasons for my opinion

The next step is to decide on an opinion about the subject. Should the new space be used for sports? Or, should it be used for the arts?

Mariah decided on her opinion. Next, she used a graphic organizer to plan her writing. She wrote her opinion. Then she wrote down reasons and facts that supported her opinion. Here is the organizer Mariah used:

Read
Note
**Organize**

| **My Opinion: We should build an arts center.** |
|---|
| **Reason/Fact 1:** We already have a gymnasium. Sports teams have a place to practice. |
| **Reason/Fact 2:** We need space to put on plays. The cafeteria has only a small area for plays. We can hardly ever rehearse there because the space is used for lunch and for lunch cleanup. |
| **Reason/Fact 3:** |

What is another fact that Mariah could add to the chart?

_____

_____

_____

✔ Mariah thinks the space should be used for the arts center. She needs to give another reason that supports this. Here is a sample answer:

Students have no place to have art classes or put on plays. If we have a good space for the arts, more kids will do art activities.

Now Mariah is ready to write her draft.

## Step 2: Drafting

**Read Mariah's draft. Then answer the questions.**

Our school is building a new space that I think we should use four a arts center. We alredy have a big gym. The sports teams have a good space to practice. they even have a locker room. There no place for kids who want to learn about art. A theater is a good place to have plays. The cafeteria is the only place to put on plays and it is two small and busy. When we get a new space, we should make an arts center with a theater. They can take art and dance classes. That way, all students in our school has a place to do what they like the best.

What is the topic sentence in the paragraph?

_____

_____

✓ **The topic sentence is the main point of the paragraph. How do you know what Mariah's paper is about? Here is a sample answer:**

_Mariah tells the reader what her paper is about in the first sentence. This is the topic sentence._

How many facts or reasons does Mariah use to support her opinion?

   **A** one

   **B** two

   **C** three

   **D** four

✓ **Mariah uses three facts or reasons. Choice C is the correct answer.**

What is a fact or reason she gives to support her opinion?

_____

_____

✓ **A fact or reason is a statement that can be proven. Here is a sample answer:**

_The school already has a big gym._

Now, Mariah is ready to revise her draft.

# Step 3: Revising

Our school is building a new space that I think we
should use four a arts center. We alrєady have a big gym.
The sports teams have a good space to practice. they even
have a locker room. There no place for kids who want to
learn about art. ~~A theater is a good place to have plays.~~
The cafeteria is the only place to put on plays, and it
is two small and busy. When we get a new space, we should
make an arts center with a theater. for kids to put on plays They can take art
and dance classes. there, too. That way, all students in our school
have ~~has~~ a place to do what they like the best.

Why did Mariah cross out a sentence?

_____

_____

_____

_____

✔ Facts and reasons are used to support an opinion. These can be proved. An opinion is something that someone thinks or believes. Some words give clues to opinions. These words are: *think, feel, believe, seem.* They are also words like *everyone, best, worst, always, never,* and *nobody.* Here is a sample answer:

> This sentence is an opinion. The word *good* is a clue that this is an opinion. Not everyone may think this is good. Mariah took out the sentence because it did not give a fact or reason for her opinion.

Why did she add words to sentence 7?

_____

_____

_____

✔ Sometimes writers rewrite sentences to make their meaning clearer. Or, they rewrite sentences to give more information. Here is a sample answer:

> Theaters can also be used to watch movies. Mariah added these words to make it clear that the theater would be used for plays.

What is her concluding sentence?

_____

_____

✓ An argument begins with an opinion. The other sentences support the opinion. Then the concluding sentence sums up the writer's main point. Or, it offers additional support. Here is a sample response:

Mariah's concluding sentence is, "That way, all students in our school have a place to do what they like the best."

# Peer Review

Mariah used this rubric to review her writing. Then she exchanged papers with another student. They reviewed each other's writing and gave it a score based on the rubric. Then they discussed ways they could improve their writing.

## Checklist for Writing Opinions and Facts

**Score 3**
- The writing answers all parts of the question.
- The paragraph starts with a topic sentence that tells the writer's opinion.
- There are at least three good reasons given for the opinion.
- The writer uses many important facts to support the opinion.
- Capitalization and punctuation are correct.

**Score 2**
- The writing answers almost all parts of the question.
- The topic sentence does not tell the writer's opinion.
- There are at least two good reasons given for the opinion.
- The writer uses a few important facts.
- There are some mistakes in capitalization and punctuation.

**Score 1**
- The writing answers only part of the question.
- There is no clear topic sentence.
- The reasons given for the opinion are hard to understand.
- The writer does not include enough facts to support the opinion.
- There are many mistakes in capitalization and punctuation.

Once Mariah has revised her paper and is happy with it, her next step is to edit her paper.

# Step 4: Editing

_____

_____

_____

_____

> During the editing stage, a writer corrects mistakes. These might be mistakes in spelling, capitalization, or punctuation. Here is a sample response:

*She changed the word four to for in sentence 1.*

*She capitalized the word they in sentence 4.*

*She added the word is after There in sentence 5.*

*She changed the word two in sentence 6. It should be too.*

# Step 5: Publishing

The final step is for Mariah to publish her writing. There are many ways to publish something. Mariah could make a PowerPoint presentation. Or, she could read her writing to the class.

How will Mariah publish her writing?

   **A**  She will read it to the class.

   **B**  She will turn it into her teacher.

   **C**  She will make a PowerPoint presentation.

   **D**  She will send it to the editor of the school newsletter.

> Choices A, B, and C are good ways for Mariah to publish her writing. However, the assignment said that she was to "write an article for the school's newsletter." The correct answer is choice D.

# Test Yourself

## Frequently Asked Questions About Health and Exercise for Kids

**Q. Why do I need to exercise?**

**A.** Exercise is important for staying healthy. Exercise helps you feel stronger. It also helps you look your best. It seems funny, but when you don't exercise, you get tired more easily! People who exercise have more energy to do the things they want to do.

**Q. What if I don't like sports?**

**A.** You don't have to play a sport to exercise. You can take walks, or ride your bike. You can hike with your family and friends. You can even build a snow fort—and that's not just exercise, it's fun! Try to think of sports that are a bit unusual. What about rock climbing or skateboarding? No matter what exercise you choose, it's more fun to do it with friends.

**Q. Why is breakfast important?**

**A.** You will often hear that breakfast is the most important meal of the day. It's true! Your body has been without food all night. It needs energy in the morning, more than any other time of day. Maybe you don't have time to sit down for a plateful of eggs or even a bowl of cereal. So, grab a peanut butter sandwich instead! Make sure, whatever you do, that you don't skip this very important meal.

**Q. Do I have to stop eating fast food to be healthy?**

**A.** No one food is bad. You just have to eat less of some foods to have energy. Foods like hamburgers and fries are okay once in a while. But whole grains, lean meats, fruits, and vegetables give you more energy. A balanced diet is a good diet!

People are always talking about healthy diets and exercise. Many adults exercise at health clubs. Some people join running clubs. Others climb mountains together. But what about children? Do they need their own exercise programs? Write an article for your student newspaper to give your opinion. Be sure to:

- include a topic sentence that tells your opinion
- give at least three good reasons or facts for your opinion
- write this article for the students who will read your school newspaper

**1** Who is your audience?

_____

_____

_____

_____

Read

Note

Organize

**2** What kind of writing are you being asked to do?

_____

_____

_____

_____

_____

**3** Fill in the opinion and reason/fact graphic organizer to plan your writing.

| My Opinion: |
| --- |
| Reason/Fact 1: |
| Reason/Fact 2: |
| Reason/Fact 3: |

**UNIT 2** ✖✖✖✖✖✖✖✖✖✖✖✖✖✖✖✖✖✖✖✖✖✖✖✖✖✖✖✖✖
**Types of Writing**

**4** Use the organizer to help you write your draft below. Be sure your topic sentence gives your opinion. Then write each fact or reason for your opinion.

_____

_____

_____

_____

_____

_____

_____

_____

_____

_____

_____

_____

_____

_____

_____

_____

_____

_____

**5** When you have finished your draft, go back over it. Make your revisions on this page. Then edit your draft. Use the rubric on page 92 to review your writing. Have a peer edit your writing if appropriate.

_____

_____

_____

_____

_____

_____

_____

_____

_____

_____

_____

_____

_____

_____

_____

_____

**6** Write your final copy on this page. Publish it by showing it to your teacher.

_____

_____

_____

_____

_____

_____

_____

_____

_____

_____

_____

_____

_____

_____

_____

_____

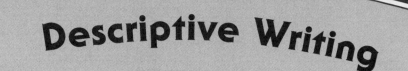

# Descriptive Writing

W.3.2. 4–6, 8, 9

**Descriptive writing** is writing to "paint a picture." You are writing to describe a person, place, or thing. You do this by picking the details that give the best picture of your subject. These details relate to the senses. You might describe what you see, taste, feel, touch, or hear. Maybe, you are describing your bedroom. You might use details that tell the colors of your room or the feel of your carpet or floor.

The topic sentence in a descriptive paragraph tells the subject. The other sentences give details. The last sentence tells how you feel about the subject.

## Guided Practice

**Read the question. Then write a response.**

You have been asked to write a paragraph for your class newsletter about a restaurant you have visited. Use details to describe this place and bring it to life. Talk about what it looks like, sounds like, smells like, and feels like. Be sure to:

- use details that make readers feel as if they are at the place
- arrange your details in an order that makes sense

**UNIT 2**
Types of Writing

# Step 1: Prewriting

What will you be writing about?

_____

_____

_____

_____

_____

✓ Think about the question. Look for clues that tell what you will be writing. Who is the audience? What type of writing are you asked to do? What is the subject?

The words *use details to describe* tell you to write a descriptive paragraph. The words *about a restaurant you have visited* tell you to write about your own experience. Finally, the words *for your class* tell you that your audience is students your age.

Step 1: Prewriting

The next step is to plan what you will write. You can use a graphic organizer to put your thoughts in order.

What type of graphic organizer would you use?

**A** timeline

**B** five senses web

**C** Venn diagram

**D** compare and contrast chart

> Think about what type of graphic organizer will work well for the writing you must do. Timelines show the order in which things happened. A Venn diagram and a compare and contrast chart show what is the same and what is different between two things. Choices A, C, and D are incorrect. Choice B is the correct answer. A five senses web helps you think about sensory details.

Here is a five senses web that one student, Jayden, used. He included details about what the place looks like, smells like, sounds like, and feels like.

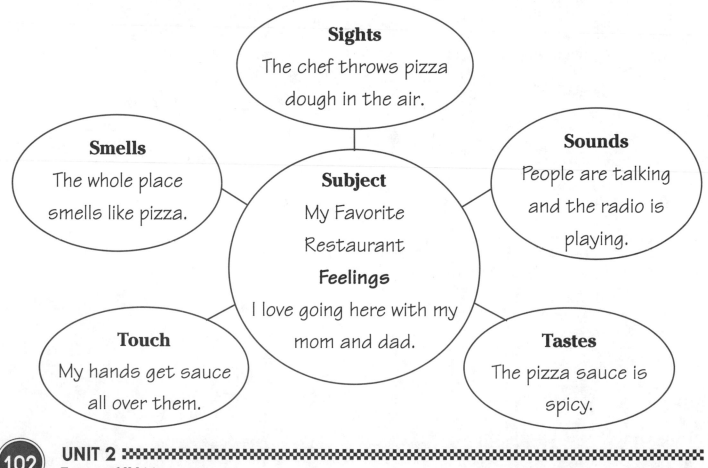

**Sights**
The chef throws pizza dough in the air.

**Smells**
The whole place smells like pizza.

**Sounds**
People are talking and the radio is playing.

**Subject**
My Favorite Restaurant
**Feelings**
I love going here with my mom and dad.

**Touch**
My hands get sauce all over them.

**Tastes**
The pizza sauce is spicy.

Which sense *best* describes the detail?

The dog's fur felt soft.

   **A**  sight

   **B**  smell

   **C**  sound

   **D**  touch

> Choice D is the correct answer. This detail is about the sense of touch. Choices A, B, and C are incorrect.

The mushrooms tasted bitter.

   **A**  sight

   **B**  smell

   **C**  taste

   **D**  touch

> Choice C is the correct answer. This detail is about the sense of taste. Choices A, B, and D are incorrect.

The walls in her bedroom were blue.

   **A**  sight

   **B**  smell

   **C**  sound

   **D**  touch

> Choice A is the correct answer. This detail is about the sense of sight. Choices B, C, and D are incorrect.

Once you've developed a plan, the next step is to write your draft.

# Step 2: Drafting

My favorite restaurant is Prato. It's a pizza place the chef throws pizza dough in the air and you can watch him cook. It's loud and you can hear people taking all the time. The radio plays old songs. The whole place smell like pizza it makes me hungry.

We get the tomato pizza. I have to be carful not to burn my mouth. The pizza sauce is spicy. The crust is very crunchy I always get my hands messy. I love going here with my mom and dad. we go every friday.

What is Jayden's topic sentence?

_____

_____

✓ Think about the details Jayden uses. What is the main idea they support? Here's a sample response:

Jayden's topic sentence is, "My favorite restaurant is Prato."

What words does Jayden use to describe tastes?

_____

✓ Good writers use descriptive words. These words let the reader experience what something feels like or what it tastes like. Here is a sample answer:

spicy, crunchy, burn

What words does Jayden use to describe sounds?

_____

✓ Adjectives often help the reader recognize how something might feel or taste. Describing actions can also help a reader understand what something looks like or what it sounds like. Here is a sample answer:

loud, talking all the time, plays old songs

Jayden's next step is to revise his draft.

## Step 3: Revising

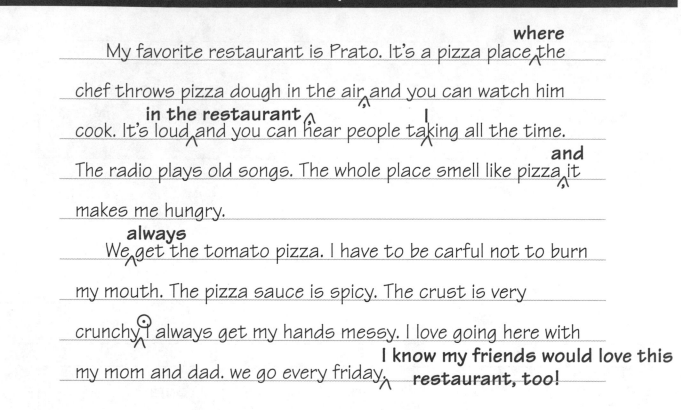

My favorite restaurant is Prato. It's a pizza place ∧*where* the

chef throws pizza dough in the air ∧and you can watch him

cook. It's loud ∧*in the restaurant* and you can hear people taking all the time. ∧*I*

The radio plays old songs. The whole place smell like pizza ∧*and* it

makes me hungry.

*always*

We ∧get the tomato pizza. I have to be carful not to burn

my mouth. The pizza sauce is spicy. The crust is very

crunchy ∧ I always get my hands messy. I love going here with

my mom and dad. we go every friday ∧ *I know my friends would love this restaurant, too!*

Why did Jayden add the word *where* to sentence 2?

_____

_____

✓ Think about the second sentence. Is the meaning clear to the reader? Is it a complete sentence? Here's a sample answer:

Jayden added the word *where* to make this sentence a complete sentence.

Why did Jayden add a sentence to the end of the paragraph?

_____

_____

✔ Think about the elements in a paragraph essay. Does this paragraph have an introduction, topic sentence, supporting details, and concluding sentence? Here's a sample answer:

_The new sentence sums up Jayden's feelings about the_
_restaurant Prato._

## Peer Review

Jayden used this checklist to review his writing. This checklist is also called a **rubric.** Then he exchanged papers with another student. They reviewed each other's writing and gave it a score based on the rubric. Then they discussed ways they could improve their writing.

# Checklist for Descriptive Writing

**Score 3**
- The writing answers all parts of the question.
- The topic sentence clearly describes the subject.
- The writing brings the subject to life by using details related to the five senses.
- The last sentence gives a clear feeling about the subject.
- Words are used correctly and well.
- There are almost no mistakes in grammar, capitalization, punctuation, and spelling.

**Score 2**
- The writing answers almost all parts of the question.
- The topic sentence describes the subject, but could be clearer.
- The writing uses some details related to the five senses.
- The last sentence gives a somewhat clear feeling about the subject.
- Some words are misused.
- There are some mistakes in grammar, capitalization, punctuation, and spelling.

**Score 1**
- The writing answers only part of the question.
- The topic sentence is missing or unclear.
- Most of the details don't come from describing the senses.
- The last sentence does not give a clear feeling about the subject.
- Many words are overused or misused.
- There are several mistakes in grammar, capitalization, punctuation, and spelling.

Now, Jayden is ready to edit his paper.

**UNIT 2** ▦▦▦▦▦▦▦▦▦▦▦▦▦▦▦▦▦▦▦▦▦▦▦▦▦▦▦▦▦▦▦▦▦▦▦▦
Types of Writing

## Step 4: Editing

Reread Jayden's draft on page 106. Then find and correct four more errors.

_____

_____

_____

_____

✔ Did you find all the errors in punctuation, spelling, and usage? Here's a sample answer:

*Change smell to smells in sentence 5.*
*Change carful to careful in sentence 7.*
*Change the word we to We in sentence 12.*
*Change the word friday to Friday in sentence 12.*

## Step 5: Publishing

The last step is for Jayden to share his work. He can do this by handwriting his work. He is going to put it in the class newsletter. The best way to publish it is to use a computer. Then he can email it to the editor. He can also give the editor a printout.

# Test Yourself

Karim is going to summer camp for a week. He has made a list of what to pack.

## What I Need for Camp

| | |
|---|---|
| sleeping bag | baseball |
| 3 pairs jeans | baseball glove |
| 3 pairs shorts | bug spray |
| 7 pairs underwear | sneakers |
| 7 pairs socks | hiking boots |
| 7 T-shirts | comic books |
| toothbrush | flashlight |
| toothpaste | notebook |
| comb | pens |
| shampoo | hat |
| soap in a dish | sunscreen |
| lifejacket | small backpack |
| swimming trunks | |

Think of what it might be like to go to Karim's summer camp. Write a paragraph that describes one activity he experienced at camp. Use details from this packing list to help you make a clear picture. Be sure to:

- describe the details using words related to the five senses
- write a topic sentence that tells the subject
- use a last sentence that gives a clear feeling about the subject

**1** What kind of writing are you being asked to do? How do you know?

Read
Note
Organize

_____

_____

_____

_____

_____

**2** What subject is the question asking you to write about?

Read
**Note**
Organize

_____

_____

_____

_____

_____

**3** Reread the list of items and the question. Then write a descriptive paragraph about an activity that Karim experienced at camp. Use the five senses web to help you plan your writing.

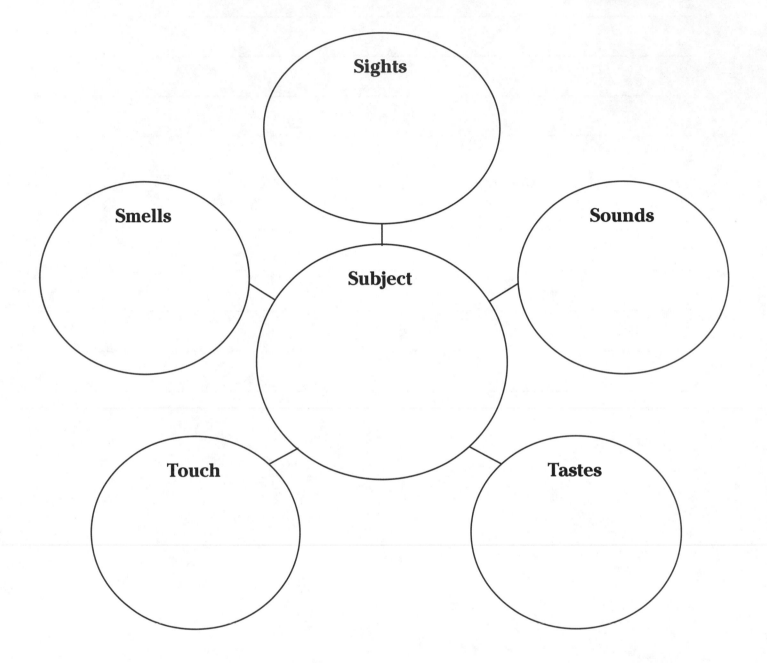

**4** Write a draft. First, look at the web. Think about how the topic sentence talks about the subject. Think about the details that support the subject. Do the details make readers feel like they are there? Make sure to use interesting words.

_____

_____

_____

_____

_____

_____

_____

_____

_____

_____

_____

_____

_____

**5** When you have finished your draft, go back over it. Make your revisions below. Then edit the draft. Use the rubric on page 108 to review the paper. Ask a peer to edit it if appropriate.

_____

_____

_____

_____

_____

_____

_____

_____

_____

_____

_____

_____

_____

_____

_____

**UNIT 2** ▨▨▨▨▨▨▨▨▨▨▨▨▨▨▨▨▨▨▨▨▨▨▨▨▨▨▨▨▨▨▨▨▨▨▨▨▨▨▨▨▨▨
Types of Writing

**6** Write your final copy on this page. Publish your work by
showing it to your teacher.

_____

_____

_____

_____

_____

_____

_____

_____

_____

_____

_____

_____

_____

_____

# Narrative Writing

W.3.3–6

When you write a story, you need a beginning, middle, and end. A story can be based on events that happened in real life. Or, a story can be made up. This is called **creative writing.** You can put real life events in a made-up story to make it seem real. When you write a story about you, use the pronouns *I* and *me*. This is called a first-person narrative.

The events and details in the story should be written in the order that they really happened. This is called **time order.** Using time order gives the story a clear beginning, middle, and end.

## Guided Practice

**Read the question. Then answer the questions.**

> Write a story for first graders at your school about your first day in first grade.
> Be sure to:
> - give details about your school, your teacher, and other students
> - write details that tell what you remember from this day
> - put details in the order in which they happened
> - use one paragraph

# Step 1: Prewriting

Read the question carefully. What words give clues about what you are being asked to write?

_____

_____

_____

_____

✓ **Think about who you are writing for, and what you are writing. How long should your writing be? Here is a sample answer:**

> *Story tells you the kind of writing you will do. First graders tells who you are writing for. The subject is the first day of first grade. The story should be one paragraph. The story also should be in the order in which events happened.*

What are two ways to learn how a character feels about something?

_____

_____

_____

✓ **The reader wants to know more about the main character. Think about the stories you have read. How did you find out what the character was thinking or feeling? Here is a sample answer:**

> *The main character can tell you with his thoughts or words. Or, other characters in the story can tell you. A narrator can tell you, too.*

The next step is to plan what you will write. A graphic organizer helps you write down your ideas. Think about the writing you will do. Then think about what kind of graphic organizer fits the kind of writing you will do. One student, Carla, used a timeline to put the details of her story in the order they happened.

**Subject:** My First Day in First Grade

| **1** | **3** | **5** |
|---|---|---|
| I wore a blue dress with a cat on the front pocket. | My mother waited at the bus stop with me. | A fifth grader helped me. |

| **2** | **4** |
|---|---|
| I was too scared to eat my cereal. | I got lost in the hallway. |

Look at the sentences below. Number them in the order in which you think they happened. Number them 6, 7, 8, and 9 to complete the timeline on the previous page.

_____ Next, Mrs. Rosencrantz gave us new pencils and a notebook.

_____ At lunch, I spilled milk on my dress by accident.

_____ First, my teacher told us her name was Mrs. Rosencrantz.

_____ We played counting games after lunch and recess.

✓ **Think about the clues in the sentence. What happened first, next, and last? Think about when the event happened. Was it before or after another event? The events were in this order:**

_____7_____ Next, Mrs. Rosencrantz gave us new pencils and a notebook.

_____8_____ At lunch, I spilled milk on my dress by accident.

_____6_____ First, my teacher told us her name was Mrs. Rosencrantz.

_____9_____ We played counting games after lunch and recess.

Once you have written a plan, the next step is to write a first draft.

## Step 2: Drafting

I remeber my first day. My first day of school. I wore a blue dresses with a cat on it. I was too scared to eat my cereal. "I am scared about school," I said. My mom gave me a hug. "Carla, you will do just fine. The other children feel the same way!" My mother she waited at the bus stop with me. I got lost in the hallway. Because it was my first day. a girl in the fifth grade took me to my classroom. First, my teacher told my class her name was Mrs. Rosencrantz. She liked cats. and Mrs. Rosencrantz gave us new pencils and a notebook. We wrote some new words, we went the cafeteria to eat lunch I spilled milk on my dress by accident. Then the bus came to take me home. We played counting games after recess. I loved school but I was vary tired I took a nap.

What is the first detail Carla wrote about?

_____

_____

✔ Details help the reader become interested in the story. They also give information about when events happened. Think about what Carla wrote in her first sentences. Here is a sample answer:

what she wore the first day of school

How do you know what Carla was feeling before she went to school?

_____

_____

> ✔ Think about the words the characters speak. This is called dialogue. Also, think about what Carla reveals about her thoughts and feelings. Here is a sample answer.

Carla wrote that she was scared. She also told her mother that she was scared.

What is the last detail she wrote about?

_____

_____

> ✔ Carla's last sentence explains what she did after school. How did she feel about school? Here is a sample answer:

She loved school, but she was very tired and took a nap.

Once the draft is written, the next step is to revise it.

# Step 3: Revising

**Read Carla's revised draft. Then answer the questions.**

I remember my first day. ~~My first day of school.~~ (in first grade) I wore a
new blue dresses with a cat on ~~it.~~ the pocket I was too scared that morning to eat my
cereal. "I am scared about school," I said. My mom gave me
a hug. "Carla, you will do just fine. The other children feel the
same way!" My mother ~~she~~ waited at the bus stop with me.
After I got to school I got lost in the hallway. ~~Because it was my first day,~~ a
girl in the fifth grade took me to my classroom. Everyone was already there. First, my
teacher told my class her name was Mrs. Rosencrantz. ~~She~~
~~liked cats~~ and ~~Mrs. Rosencrantz~~ She gave us new pencils and a
notebook. We wrote some new words. Later we went to the cafeteria
to eat lunch I spilled milk on my dress by accident.
Then the bus came to take me home. We played counting games
after recess. I loved school but I was vary tired. I took a nap when I got home.

What words or groups of words did Carla add to show time order?

_____

_____

Some words give clues about when something happened. Words like *first, then,* and *now* are examples of this type of words. Think about the words Carla used in her story. How did you know what happened in the beginning, the middle, and the end of the story? Here is a sample answer:

____In first grade, that morning, After I got to school,____
____already there, Later, when I got home_____

Why did Carla cross out the sentence about cats?

_____

_____

Do you know what details to put into a story? Do you know which ones to leave out? Some details are important to what happens in the story. Other details do not add anything. Here is a sample answer:

____It isn't an important detail._____

## Peer Review

When the draft is revised, the next step is to make sure it fits the checklist, or rubric. Carla used the rubric to review her writing. Then she exchanged papers with another student. They reviewed each other's writing and gave it a score based on the rubric. Then they discussed ways they could improve their writing.

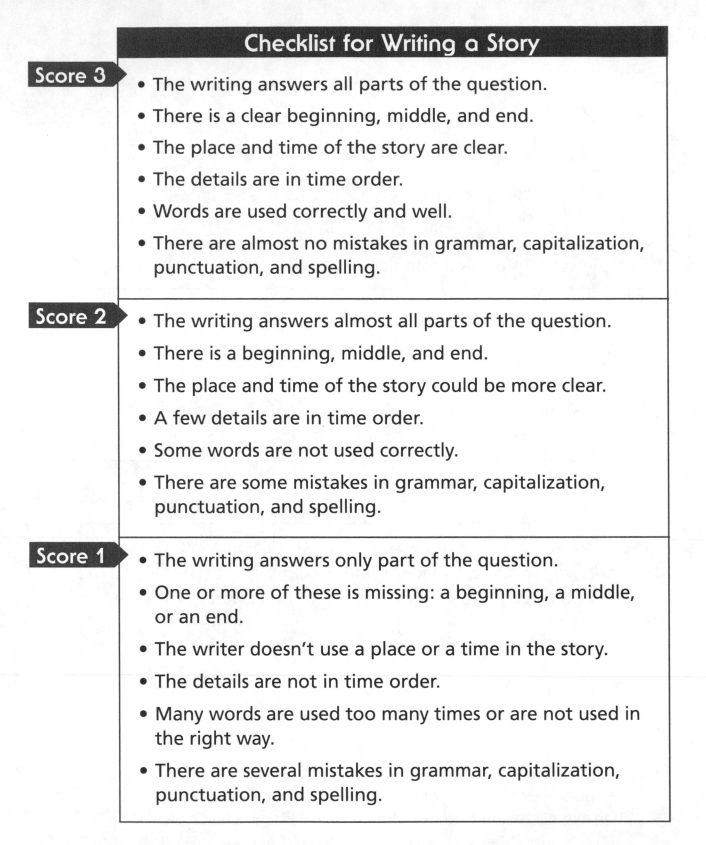

## Checklist for Writing a Story

**Score 3**

- The writing answers all parts of the question.
- There is a clear beginning, middle, and end.
- The place and time of the story are clear.
- The details are in time order.
- Words are used correctly and well.
- There are almost no mistakes in grammar, capitalization, punctuation, and spelling.

**Score 2**

- The writing answers almost all parts of the question.
- There is a beginning, middle, and end.
- The place and time of the story could be more clear.
- A few details are in time order.
- Some words are not used correctly.
- There are some mistakes in grammar, capitalization, punctuation, and spelling.

**Score 1**

- The writing answers only part of the question.
- One or more of these is missing: a beginning, a middle, or an end.
- The writer doesn't use a place or a time in the story.
- The details are not in time order.
- Many words are used too many times or are not used in the right way.
- There are several mistakes in grammar, capitalization, punctuation, and spelling.

Carla is ready to edit her paper.

# Step 4: Editing

Why did Carla capitalize the letter a in sentence 11?

    **A**  It is the beginning of a sentence.

    **B**  It is the teacher's name.

    **C**  It is the name of the school.

    **D**  It is the name of a classmate.

> **Choice A is the correct answer. Carla has made a new sentence. Choices B, C, and D are also examples of when to use capitalization. They are incorrect answers for sentence 11.**

Find and correct three more errors in Carla's draft.

_____

_____

_____

> **Look for words that are misspelled. Make sure that the correct punctuation is used. Did you find all the errors? Here is a sample answer:**

    *In sentence 3, change dresses to dress.*
    *In sentence 14, add a period after the word lunch.*
    *In sentence 17, change vary to very.*

# Step 5: Publish

    The last step is to publish what is written. There are many ways to publish creative writing. Carla can use a computer to create her paper and then print it out. After she turns it in, she may be asked to read it to the class. Her teacher might also read it to the class. Carla could even enter it into a writing contest.

# Test Yourself

## Local Girl and Her Dog Are Winners

Ariel Gilbert started running in the Henryville 5K Spring Race when she was 10 years old. Now she is 15 years old. Ariel never won the race, but she always felt like a winner. Why? Ariel Gilbert is blind.

Everyone told Ariel she could not run in a race. But Ariel wanted to run. When she ran, her faithful guide dog led the way. Ariel knew that she could finish a race with the help of her dog Bruno. Luckily, Bruno is quite a runner! Every year both Ariel and her dog have crossed the finish line at Henryville. But Saturday's Henryville 5K Spring Race was different. This time, Ariel was ready to win.

This year, Ariel tried out for her school track team. The coach let Bruno run with Ariel. She ran in cross-country races. Bruno ran with her. They both trained hard. In Saturday's race, her dream came true. Ariel Gilbert was the first blind runner to win the Henryville 5K.

**1** What event does this article talk about?

_____

_____

_____

_____

**2** What are some of the details?

_____

_____

_____

_____

 **126** UNIT 2 ▒▒▒▒▒▒▒▒▒▒▒▒▒▒▒▒▒▒▒▒▒▒▒▒▒▒▒▒▒▒▒▒▒▒▒▒
**Types of Writing**

Pretend that you were at the Henryville 5K Spring Race. Write a story about Ariel winning the race.
In your story, be sure to:

- write events in the order that they happened
- use details that make the story seem real
- write about the place and the time of the story

**3** What kind of writing are you being asked to do?

_____

_____

_____

_____

**Read**
Note
Organize

**4** Who are you writing for?

_____

_____

_____

_____

Read
**Note**
Organize

**5** Fill in the chart to help answer the question and arrange the events in time order.

Read
Note
**Organize**

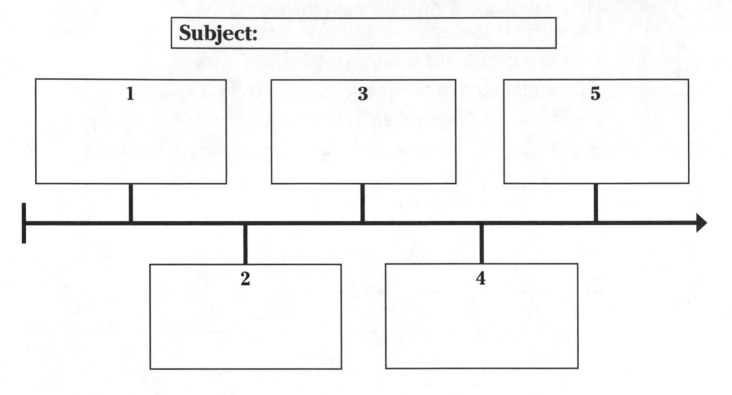

| Subject: |
|---|

```
    ┌───────────┐      ┌───────────┐      ┌───────────┐
    │     1     │      │     3     │      │     5     │
    │           │      │           │      │           │
    └─────┬─────┘      └─────┬─────┘      └─────┬─────┘
          │                  │                  │
  ────────┼──────────┬───────┼──────────┬───────┼────────▶
                     │                  │
              ┌──────┴────┐      ┌──────┴────┐
              │     2     │      │     4     │
              │           │      │           │
              └───────────┘      └───────────┘
```

**UNIT 2**
**Types of Writing**

**6** Write your draft. First, look at the timeline. Think about the main subject of your paragraph. Did you write the details in time order? Remember to use words that make your story interesting.

**7** When you have finished your draft, go back over it. Make your changes on this page. Edit your draft. Use the rubric on page 124 to review your paper. Have a peer edit your paragraph if appropriate.

_____

_____

_____

_____

_____

_____

_____

_____

_____

_____

_____

_____

_____

_____

**8** Write your final copy on the lines below. Publish it by
showing your work to your teacher.

_____

_____

_____

_____

_____

_____

_____

_____

_____

_____

_____

_____

_____

_____

# Informational Writing

**W.3.2, 4–6, 8, 9**

When you write a report, you are doing **informational writing.** This type of writing tells the facts. You use this kind of writing to answer a question on a test. You also use it to write a report. This is the writing you do most often in class.

Informational writing needs to be well organized. There are many ways you can organize it. One way is to use cause and effect. Or, you can use main idea and detail. Another way is to use sequence. Step-by-step directions are organized in order, or sequence. The steps must be in the right order or the directions won't work.

## Guided Practice

**Read the assignment. Then answer the questions.**

> When the fire alarm rings in your school, what do you do? How do you get out of the building? What are your school's rules for fire drills? Tell a student who is new to your class what to do in a fire drill. Write a paper with directions for this student.
>
> Be sure to:
> - put the steps in order
> - write all the steps you usually follow
> - write one paragraph

# Step 1: Prewriting

Here's how one student, Nico, began the assignment. First, he read the question. Then he underlined key words.

What words told Nico what he should do for this assignment?

_____

_____

_____

_____

_____

_____

✓ The assignment should tell you who the audience is. It should tell you what the purpose is. You also need to know the format of the assignment. Here is a sample answer:

Nico probably underlined directions. This tells him the type of writing he must do. He must explain how to do something. Steps and order tell him that he needs to use sequence to organize his writing. He knows he must tell what happened first, next, and last. He also underlined paragraph. This tells how long the assignment should be.

The next step before writing is to make a plan. A plan helps you know what you will write and how you will organize it. A graphic organizer can help you plan what you will write. Nico decided to use a sequence chart. This will help him put the steps in the right order.

| What We Do in a Fire Drill | |
| --- | --- |
| Step 1 | First, the alarm rings. |
| Step 2 | Then the teacher tells us to line up at the door. |
| Step 3 | We can't take anything with us. We just go. |
| Step 4 | |
| Step 5 | |
| Step 6 | |

Read the steps below. Which ones complete the chart above? Label your choices Step 4, Step 5, and Step 6 in that order.

_____ The teacher calls our names to see if we all got out of the school.

_____ We read about the fire station.

_____ Then we march in a line to the exit.

_____ We go back inside when the fire chief says it's okay.

What should you do first? What should you do next? Knowing what to do when is important. Steps need to be done in the right sequence if the fire drill is to be a success. Here is a sample answer:

| | |
|---|---|
| <u>   Step 5   </u> | The teacher calls our names to see if we all got out of the school. |
| <u>           </u> | We read about the fire station. |
| <u>   Step 4   </u> | Then we march in a line to the exit. |
| <u>   Step 6   </u> | We go back inside when the fire chief says it's okay. |

Nico finished his plan. He is ready to start writing.

## Step 2: Drafting

**Read the draft. Then answer the questions.**

Here's what we do in a fire drill at our school. First, the alarm rings then the teacher tells us to line up at the door. We cant take anything with us. We don't take our books. We just have go fast. Then we march in a line. We go to the exit. The teacher calls our name to see if we all there. Then we go back in when the fire cheif says its okay.

What did Nico explain in his draft?

_____

_____

✔ Nico is writing important directions. Here is a sample answer:

Nico explained what rules to follow in a school fire drill.

What connecting words did Nico use?

_____

_____

> Connecting words are words that signal how things are related. These words can be *first, second,* and *third.* Or, they might be other words related to sequence. Did Nico use any words that signal time order? Here is a sample answer:

First, Then, when

Are the steps in the right order? How do you know?

_____

_____

> Steps need to be in the right order. This is known as chronological order or time order. Here is a sample answer:

Yes, the steps are in the right order. I know because the order makes sense.

Next, Nico will revise his writing.

**136** **UNIT 2** ▓▓▓▓▓▓▓▓▓▓▓▓▓▓▓▓▓▓▓▓▓▓▓▓▓▓▓▓▓▓▓▓▓▓▓▓▓
Types of Writing

# Step 3: Revising

**Read Nico's revised draft. Then answer the questions.**

Here's what we do in a fire drill at our school. First, the
**fire**
alarm rings⊙ then the teacher tells us to line up at the door.

We can't take anything with us. ~~We don't take our books.~~ We
**as   as we can.**
just have go fast. Then we march in a line. We go to the exit.
**We walk outside, away from the school.**                    **are**
The teacher calls our name to see if we all there. Then we go

back in when the fire cheif says it's okay.

Find the long sentence that Nico made into two sentences. Write
the two sentences.

_____

_____

✓ Revising means fixing any problems with your writing. This
might mean rewriting long run-on sentences. Or, it might mean
combining short sentences with the same information. Here is a
sample answer:

First, the fire alarm rings. Then the teacher tells us to
line up at the door.

Which sentence did Nico cross out?

_____

_____

✓ Think about the proofreading symbols you learned in Lesson 1. The delete symbol means to take out. Look for the delete symbol in the revised draft. Here is a sample answer:

Nico crossed out the sentence, "We don't take our books."

Why did he cross it out?

_____

_____

✓ Informational writing is clear and direct. Only the most important details are included. Each detail should add new information. Here is a sample answer:

The sentence doesn't tell anything important. The sentence before it already told us that we can't take anything. We already know we can't take our books.

## Peer Review

Nico used this checklist to review his writing. Then he exchanged papers with another student. They reviewed each other's writing and gave it a score based on the rubric. Then they discussed ways they could improve their writing.

**138** UNIT 2 :::::::::::::::::::::::::::::::::::::::::::::::::::::::::::::::::::
Types of Writing

# Checklist for Informational Writing

**Score 3**
- The writing answers all parts of the question.
- There is a topic sentence with a clear main idea.
- All details support the main idea.
- Connecting words connect facts and events in the right time order.
- Words are used correctly and well.
- There are almost no mistakes in grammar, capitalization, punctuation, and spelling.

**Score 2**
- The writing answers almost all parts of the question.
- The topic sentence states the main idea, but could be stronger.
- Most details support the main idea, but some do not belong.
- Some connecting words connect facts and events in the right time order.
- Some words are not used correctly.
- There are some mistakes in grammar, capitalization, punctuation, and spelling.

**Score 1**
- The writing answers only part of the question.
- The topic sentence is missing or unclear.
- Some details are confusing or do not belong.
- Few connecting words connect facts and events in the right time order.
- Many words are not used correctly.
- There are many mistakes in grammar, capitalization, punctuation, and spelling.

Now, Nico can edit his paper.

## Step 4: Editing

**Proofread Nico's revised draft on page 137. Find and correct three more mistakes.**

_____

_____

_____

✓ Did Nico have any misspelled words? Did he use the correct punctuation marks? These are mistakes to look for when editing. Here is a sample answer:

In sentence 5, insert the word *to* between *have* and *go*

In sentence 9, change the word *name* to *names*

In sentence 10, change the word *cheif* to *chief*

## Step 5: Publishing

The last step is to publish your writing. Nico can do this by turning his paper into this teacher. His teacher may ask the students to make a poster of the steps to display in the classroom. This is another way to publish your writing.

## Who Wrote the First Computer Program?

The answer to this question surprises a lot of people. The first person to write a computer program was a woman named Ada Byron. She was born in London, England, in 1815. Her father was the famous poet, Lord Byron. He left the family when Ada was a few weeks old and never saw her again.

Ada's mother thought it would be good for Ada to study math. She didn't want Ada to become a poet like her father. Ada also loved music and dancing. Most of all, she loved to figure out how things worked. When she was 17, Ada met Mary Sommerville. Mrs. Sommerville was a mathematician, and Ada admired her very much. The two women became good friends.

When Ada was 18, she met a man named Charles Babbage. He was an inventor. He invented a machine called an Analytical Engine. In 1843, Ada wrote a plan showing how to use Babbage's machine. She showed how it could be used for math problems. Her plan was the first program for computing. She understood how this machine worked better than anyone else. Babbage worked with Ada to find other uses for his machine.

Ada died in 1852. She is remembered for being the first computer programmer. During the 1970s, the United States Department of Defense made a computer language called ADA. It was named in honor of Ada Byron and her work in programming.

> Your teacher has asked you to write a report about Ada Byron's work. Write a paragraph that tells what Ada Byron did. Use facts from the article to tell why she is important in the history of computers and math. Be sure to:
>
> - include a topic sentence and a main idea
> - use connecting words. These are words like *first, next,* and *last.* They connect facts and events in the right time order.

**1** What kind of writing are you being asked to do? How do you know?

Read

Note

Organize

_____

_____

_____

_____

_____

**2** Who will read your writing?

_____

_____

_____

_____

_____

**UNIT 2** ▨▨▨▨▨▨▨▨▨▨▨▨▨▨▨▨▨▨▨▨▨▨▨▨▨▨▨▨▨▨▨▨▨▨▨
**Types of Writing**

**3** Use the time chart to help you plan your writing. What was the sequence of events?

| Time Chart About Ada's Life |
|---|
| 1815: |
| When Ada was 17: |
| When Ada was 18: |
| 1843: |
| 1852: |
| 1970s: |

**4** Write your draft. Before you begin, look at your time chart. Think about your topic sentence. Are all the facts and events in order? Do you need to add details? Remember to use connecting words such as *first, next, after,* and *last.*

_____

_____

_____

_____

_____

_____

_____

_____

_____

_____

_____

_____

_____

_____

_____

_____

**UNIT 2** ▨▨▨▨▨▨▨▨▨▨▨▨▨▨▨▨▨▨▨▨▨▨▨▨▨▨▨▨▨▨
**Types of Writing**

**5** When you have finished your draft, go back over it. Make your changes on this page. Edit your draft. Use the rubric on page 139 to review your work. Have a peer edit it if appropriate.

_____

_____

_____

_____

_____

_____

_____

_____

_____

_____

_____

_____

_____

_____

_____

_____

_____

**6** Publish your work by writing it on this page and then showing it to your teacher.

_____

_____

_____

_____

_____

_____

_____

_____

_____

_____

_____

_____

_____

_____

_____

_____

_____

**UNIT 2** ▓▓▓▓▓▓▓▓▓▓▓▓▓▓▓▓▓▓▓▓▓▓▓▓▓▓▓▓▓▓▓▓▓▓
Types of Writing

# Research

You know how to write responses to test questions. You also know how to write for classroom assignments. This unit looks at a different type of writing. The research paper is a report. You will learn how to find information. Then you will learn how to organize it.

- **Lesson 10** focuses on finding information and taking good research notes. Knowing where to find information is an important part of writing the research paper. This lesson will help you find information and take notes.

- **In Lesson 11,** you'll learn how to create a strong thesis statement. You'll also learn how to organize your research. An outline will help you do this.

- **Lesson 12** discusses how to write a research paper. The source list is an important part of the research paper. This lesson will help you create a source list. It will also help you pick visual aids for your paper.

# Researching Sources and Content

W.3.2, 4–9

Suppose you want to find out more facts about your state. Where would you look? You could look on the website for your state. Another place to look is in an atlas. An atlas is a book with maps of places throughout the world. A book or encyclopedia can also help you. This type of fact finding is called **researching.**

You might do research for a class assignment. Or, you might do research because you want to know more about a subject. Knowing where to find facts is an important skill to have.

After you find your information, you might be asked to share it. You can do this be writing a report. Just like other writing you do, writing a research paper is done in steps.

**Step 1:** Pick a topic.

**Step 2:** Research the topic.

**Step 3:** Develop the thesis statement.

**Step 4:** Outline the paper.

**Step 5:** Write the paper.

**Step 6:** Tell the sources.

## Step 1: Pick a Topic

Knowing what you will write about is the first step. Your teacher might give you a topic. Or, you might have to pick your own topic. You want to make sure that your topic is not too big. If the subject is too broad, it is hard to write it about it in one or two pages. For example, Mrs. Kelly wanted the class to do a research project about the 50 states. Writing about all 50 states is a big project.

Mrs. Kelly narrowed down the topic. First, she had each student pick one state to write about. Next, she gave them a list of questions to answer about each state. Some of the questions were how many people lived there, what the climate was, and when it became a state. She also told them how long their reports should be. The questions and length helped the students focus their topics so they were not so broad. You can do the same thing when you pick a topic. Keep narrowing in on the topic so it is not too broad. This makes it easier to focus your research and writing.

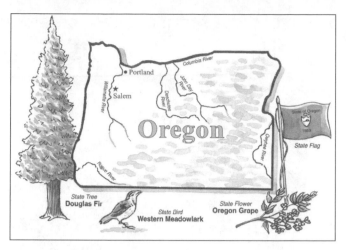

## Guided Practice

**Answer the questions.**

Which of these would make the *best* topic for a research paper?

**A** animals

**B** reptiles

**C** desert snakes

**D** diamondback snake

✓ A research paper is easier to write when the topic is focused. Choices A, B, and C are too broad. These are incorrect answers. The correct answer is choice D. This topic is the most focused of the choices.

Which of these would make the *best* topic for a research paper?

**A**  comets

**B**  space

**C**  the Milky Way galaxy

**D**  Halley's comet

> A research paper should have a focused topic. This makes the topic easier to research and write about within a certain number of pages. Choices A and B are very broad topics. Choice C is also broad. The Milky Way has many planets and stars. Choice D is the correct answer. This is the most focused topic.

## Step 2: Research the Topic

The next step is finding information about your topic. You can find information on almost any subject you can think of. You can find materials in the library, in a bookstore, in school, and on the World Wide Web.

There are many ways to find information. You could:

- ask an expert or someone who knows about the topic
- read a book about the topic
- check a website about the topic
- look in a reference book like an atlas or encyclopedia
- recall experiences

How can you use your own experiences? Maybe the topic is about an animal. You could visit the zoo to learn more the animal. If the topic is a science concept, you could do an experiment. Or, you might be asked about an activity or hobby that you know how to do. These are ways to use your own experiences.

Another important skill is knowing if the source of information can be trusted. Sometimes information can be wrong. There are some questions you can ask to help you know the difference.

- Are the facts correct? Or, are they someone's opinions?
- Is the source up to date?
- Did the person really say something? Or, did someone else say it?
- What is the source of the information?
- Who wrote the information?
- Why did they write the information?
- Do other sources agree?

Reference books are trusted sources of information. These include:

**Almanacs**—These give interesting facts about a certain year for different subjects.

**Atlases**—These contain maps of countries, states, and regions.

**Encyclopedias**—These list detailed information about all types of subjects.

Some parts of a book can also help you with your research.

The **title page** lists the name of the book and the author.

The **copyright page** tells when the book was published and the publisher. It is on the back of the title page.

A **glossary** lists key words and their meanings. It is at the back of the book.

The **table of contents** lists chapter titles in book.

An **index** lists the subjects in a book alphabetically. It also says what page tells about the subject. The index is at the back of the book, too.

A **bibliography** lists other sources related to the topic. This, too, is at the back of the book.

The table of contents is a good place to check when doing research. You can check to see if any of the chapter titles are related to your topic. If so, that chapter might have facts about your topic.

# Guided Practice

**Read the table of contents and the index. Then answer the questions.**

## Table of Contents

In which chapter would you *most likely* find information about where the inventor went to school?

**A** Chapter 1

**B** Chapter 2

**C** Chapter 3

**D** Chapter 4

Chapter 2 is about the inventor's education. This chapter will tell where the inventor went to school. Choice B is the correct answer. The other chapters are about other parts of the inventor's life. Choices A, C, and D are incorrect.

In which chapter would you *most likely* find information about the inventor's inventions?

**A** Chapter 1

**B** Chapter 2

**C** Chapter 3

**D** Chapter 4

Choices A, B, and D are about other parts of the inventor's life. They are not about his inventions. Chapter 3 has the word *inventions* as the title. Choice C is the correct answer.

**UNIT 3** ▞▞▞▞▞▞▞▞▞▞▞▞▞▞▞▞▞▞▞▞▞▞▞▞▞▞▞▞▞▞▞▞▞▞▞▞▞▞▞▞▞▞▞▞
Research

## Index

**butterflies:** types of, pages 3–4
**gardening:** pages 23–26
**habitat:** pages 5–7
**monarchs:** attracting, pages 23–26;
  life cycle of, pages 10–15;
  migration, pages 15–19;
**South America:** pages 15–19

Which pages would you read if you wanted to know where the monarch butterfly migrates to in winter?

A   pages 3–4

B   pages 5–7

C   pages 10–15

D   pages 15–19

✔  This lists the topics in a book alphabetically. You can check the index for key words that relate to your topic. Choice A is about the types of butterflies. Choice B is about their habitat. Choice C is about the life cycle of the monarch butterfly. These are incorrect. The correct answer is choice D. The index lists migration and South America as topics discussed on pages 15–19. You can guess that the monarch migrates to South America in winter.

Information can also be found online. However, not all the information online is correct. Here is a list to help you know which websites you can trust.

.edu—these websites are schools and universities
.gov—these are government websites
.org—these are organizations

Websites that end in .com are businesses. Some of these websites can be trusted to have correct information. Others may not be as trustworthy.

## Notetaking

Once you find your facts, you want to write them down. This makes it easier to write your paper. The best way to record your information is to use a note card. Write one fact on each note card.

You can **summarize** what you have read. You do this by listing the main idea and details. Or, you might **paraphrase** what you have read. This means putting the information into your own words. You should put any direct quotes in quotation marks. This helps you remember what is the author's work and what is yours.

Also, write down where you found your facts. Don't forget the page number. This helps you if you need to go back to the source. It also helps other people who want to check your source for their own research.

Here's a shortcut to keep track of your sources. You can make a list of them. Tell the title and author. Also, say who published it and when. Then give each source on the list a number. Write your fact and the number of your source on the note card. Also, write the page number where you found the information.

**UNIT 3** ▓▓▓▓▓▓▓▓▓▓▓▓▓▓▓▓▓▓▓▓▓▓▓▓▓▓▓▓▓▓▓▓▓▓▓▓▓▓▓▓▓▓▓▓
**Research**

# Guided Practice

## Source List

1 *Beautiful Butterflies* by Frank Stern.
   New York: W. W. Norton, 2007.

2 *The Migration Patterns of Monarch Butterflies* by
   Karin Kelly. New York: Facts on File, 2008.

3 *The World of Butterflies* by Pat Daniels. Washington, D.C.:
   Smith & Sons, 2006.

Fill in the note card with the number of the source where you
*most likely* found the fact.

> Source: _____
> Monarch butterflies migrate from North America
> to South America in winter.

✔ The fact on the note card is most likely from a book about the
migration of the monarch. Which book on the source list is about
migration patterns? Here is a sample answer:

> Source: 2                    Page: 10
> Monarch butterflies migrate from North America
> to South America in winter.

# Test Yourself

1 Which of the following would be a trusted reference on butterflies?

   A www.butterfliesandmore.com

   B *The Story of the Butterfly and the Bee* by Kevin James

   C Dr. Cassie Frond, butterfly expert

   D *The Life of Cassie Frond* by Mark Tully

2 Which part of a book would you check to find out about the life cycle of a butterfly?

   A copyright page

   B title page

   C index

   D glossary

3 Which of these is *not* a reference source?

   A newspaper

   B biography

   C story

   D website

4 What information should be included in a source list?

   _____

   _____

   _____

   _____

**5** What information should be included on a note card when taking notes?

_____

_____

_____

_____

_____

**6** Where would you find information about attracting butterflies to your garden?

**A** Chapter 1

**B** Chapter 3

**C** Chapter 4

**D** Chapter 5

**7** Which chapter in the table of contents is _most likely_ to have a map?

**A** Chapter 1

**B** Chapter 2

**C** Chapter 3

**D** Chapter 4

# Outlining the Research Paper

W.3.2, 4, 6–9

Picking a topic is the first step in writing a research paper. The second step is researching a topic. The next step is organizing the information.

## Step 3: Determine the Thesis Statement

The **thesis statement** sums up the main point of your paper. It tells the purpose of your paper. It is like the main idea or topic sentence that you learned about in Lesson 3. The thesis statement should be specific. It should have one main point.

This statement tells the reader what they will learn. It should appear at the end of the first paragraph. This lets the reader know what is to come in the rest of the paper.

A thesis statement should not be a fact. It should be a general statement that can be supported with facts.

# Guided Practice

Which of these is the *best* thesis statement?

**A**  My report is about a famous place.

**B**  The White House is where the president lives in Washington, D.C.

**C**  The White House in Washington, D. C. has an interesting history.

**D**  My report is about a famous building in Washington, D.C.

> Choice A is too general. Also, thesis statements do not begin with "My report is about." Choice B is a fact. Choice D is more specific. However, it begins with "My report is about." These are incorrect answers. Choice D is the correct answer. You can support this statement with facts about the building. You can also support it with facts about the presidents who lived there.

Which of these is the *best* thesis statement?

**A**  Thomas Edison lived in New Jersey.

**B**  Thomas Edison invented the lightbulb.

**C**  Thomas Edison is known as the "Wizard of Menlo Park."

**D**  Thomas Edison's inventions changed the way people lived.

> Choices A, B, and C are facts. These are incorrect. The correct answer is choice D. The author will most likely write about who Thomas Edison was and his inventions. Then the author will tell why the lightbulb and his other inventions changed the way people lived.

# Step 4: Outline the Paper

The thesis statement helps you organize your writing. Now, you know how you will sort your information. Think about the main points that support your thesis statement. Write these points down. Then sort your notes so that they match these points. Each point will become a paragraph or section in your paper.

You may find that you need more information to support a main point. If you do, then you can do more research. Or, you might find that you have too much information. If so, you leave in the most important facts. Sorting your information helps you organize your thinking. It is a road map for writing your paper.

An outline helps you sort your information. Write your main ideas down. Give them a letter. Then list details that support this idea. Give these ideas a number. Now, you have an outline to help you organize your paper.

Here's an example of this type of outline:

```
   I.   Thesis statement

  II.   Body
        A. Main Idea
           1. Detail
           2. Detail

        B. Main Idea
           1. Detail
           2. Detail

        C. Main Idea
           1. Detail
           2. Detail

 III.   Conclusion
```

Each main idea will be a paragraph in your paper. The details are the supporting sentences in the paragraph. You learned about main idea and details in Lesson 3.

# Guided Practice

---

I.   Thesis statement: Thomas Edison's inventions changed the way people lived.

II.  Body
   A. The lightbulb changed the way people lived because
     1. Detail

   B. The record player changed the way people lived because
     1. Detail

   C. The motion picture camera changed the way people lived because
     1. Detail

---

Match the statements with the main idea they support.

_____ could watch pictures that moved

_____ no longer need to burn candles to see indoors

_____ could listen to music that was recorded

✔ Each statement supports a main idea in the outline. These main ideas and details will later become paragraphs. The paragraphs support the thesis statement that Thomas Edison's inventions changed the way people lived. Here is the correct answer:

_____C_____ could watch pictures that moved

_____A_____ no longer need to burn candles to see indoors

_____B_____ could listen to music that was recorded

These facts can be sorted to match the main points of the report. If you need more facts, you can do more research. The outline for a research paper about Thomas Edison and his inventions would now look like this:

I. Thesis statement: Thomas Edison's inventions changed the way people lived.

II. Body
   A. The lightbulb changed how people lived
      1. no longer need to burn candles to see indoors
      2. today, use lightbulbs to see indoors
   B. The record player changed how people lived
      1. could listen to music that was recorded
      2. today, listen to recorded music on mp3 players
   C. The motion picture camera changed how people lived
      1. could watch pictures that moved
      2. today, watch movies in theaters and our homes

III. Conclusion: Thomas Edison invented many things. Many of them changed the way people live. Today, we still use some of these inventions.

The conclusion is the statement that sums up the purpose of the research paper. This statement is in the last paragraph.

# Test Yourself

**1** Where should the thesis statement appear in the research paper?

    **A** in the last paragraph

    **B** in every paragraph

    **C** in the second paragraph

    **D** at the end of the opening paragraph

**2** Where should the conclusion appear in the research paper?

    **A** in the last paragraph

    **B** in every paragraph

    **C** in the second paragraph

    **D** at the end of the opening paragraph

**3** What is the purpose of an outline?

_____

_____

_____

_____

**4** Read the outline. Where would you add these two details to the outline below?

      3. First Family lives in top two floors

      4. middle two floors open to the public

---

   I.   Thesis: The White House in Washington, D.C, has an interesting history.

  II.   Body
     A. president lived here since 1800
        1. John Adams first to live here
        2. George Washington didn't live here

        3. _____

        4. _____

     B. is a large building
        1. six floors
        2. famous rooms

        3. _____

        4. _____

     C. repaired many times
        1. burned during the War of 1812
        2. a piano fell through the ceiling in 1940s

        3. _____

        4. _____

 III.  Conclusion: The White House would be a very interesting place to visit.

---

**5** Using the outline, explain what you would expect to read about in paragraph 3 of the report.

_____

_____

_____

_____

_____

_____

# Writing the Research Paper

**W.3.2, 4, 6–9**

Writing a research paper uses the same writing process as the other writing that you do. Once you've finished organizing your information, you are ready to write your paper.

## Step 5: Write the Research Paper

The last step is to write your paper. You will follow the five-step writing process you learned in Lesson 1. You want to plan your paper, write your draft, then revise and edit the paper, and publish it.

You might want to include visual aids in your paper. Visual aids add interest to your paper. They help break up large areas of text. Think about what would help the reader. If you are writing about a state, a map of the whole country might be helpful. This shows where the state is located. If you are giving the reader facts and figures, a graph or chart will make this information easier to understand. A science research paper might include a diagram to help the reader.

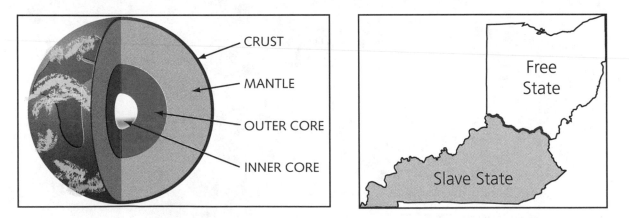

**UNIT 3**
Research

# Guided Practice

Which of the following would be helpful to show what the Red Room in the White House looks like?

**A** a floor plan

**B** a color photograph

**C** a black and white photograph

**D** a map of the grounds of the White House

> A floor plan explains where the rooms are located in a building. A black and white photograph does not show the colors used in a room. A map of the grounds tells what is outside of the White House. Choices A, C, and D are incorrect. Choice B is the correct answer. A color photograph would show what the Red Room looks like. It is called the Red Room because the ceiling, rugs, draperies, and walls are in shades of red.

What would you include in the paper to show how the White House has changed over the years?

_____

_____

_____

> Put yourself in the place of the reader. What do you want to see? How do you show how two things are different? You probably learned about differences in the White House when you did your research. Did you know the balcony was a more recent addition? Here is a sample answer:

_I would use a color photograph of the White House as it looks today. I would also use a photograph of how the White House looked at an earlier time._

# Step 6: Tell the Sources

An important part of the research paper is giving your sources. This helps readers know where you found your information. They might want to learn more about the topic. Readers can use your sources to find out more.

Readers want to know:
- where you found the information (title)
- who created it (the author and the publisher)
- when they created it (year)

The source list below from Lesson 10 gives this information.

---

## Source List

1 *Beautiful Butterflies* by Frank Stern. New York: W. W. Norton, 2007.

2 *The Migration Patterns of Monarch Butterflies* by Karin Kelly. New York: Facts on File, 2008.

3 *The World of Butterflies* by Pat Daniels. Washington, D.C.: Smith & Sons, 2006.

---

This information should also appear at the end of your paper. It is also called a **bibliography**. When these sources are used in the bibliography, they follow a certain order. The listing for a book, website, and encyclopedia should look like the examples below.

Book

Author's last name, author's first name. Title. City where published: publisher and date when published.

> Example: Stern, Frank. *Beautiful Butterflies.* New York: W. W. Norton, 2007.

Website

Title of article. Owner of website. *Retrieved* and the date you visited the website. The website address inside arrows.

Example: "Types of Butterflies." www.worldofbutterflies.com. Retrieved 6 June 2011. <www.worldofbutterflies.com>.

Encyclopedia

Entry title. Title of encyclopedia. Volume number, publication date.

Example: "Butterflies." *Encyclopedia Britannica.* Vol. 2, 2011.

The sources in a bibliography should be listed in alphabetical order by the author's last name.

## Guided Practice

**Read the questions. Then answer them.**

Why should you list the sources that you used?

_____

_____

✓ Think about how you found resources to use. Did you check the bibliographies of any books to find other sources of information? This is another good way to find information. Here is a sample answer:

To give credit to other people for their work. To help readers find information for their research.

Which of these is not included in the bibliography?

**A** author's full name

**B** date of publication

**C** city of publication

**D** number of pages in the book

You want to know who wrote a book, when it was written, and where it was published. Choices A, B, and C are incorrect. The correct answer is choice D. You do not need to include the number of pages in the book.

The complete bibliography should look like this. Note that the sources are in alphabetical order by last name. If there is no author, the source is listed alphabetically by article title. The sources are from the source list on page 168. The website and encyclopedia from page 169 are included as well.

## Bibliography

"Butterflies." *Encyclopedia Britannica.* Vol. 2, 2011.

Daniels, Pat. *The World of Butterflies.* Washington, D.C.: Smith & Sons, 2006.

Kelly, Karin. *The Migration Patterns of Monarch Butterflies.* New York: Facts on File, 2008.

Stern, Frank. *Beautiful Butterflies.* New York: W. W. Norton, 2007.

"Types of Butterflies." www.worldofbutterflies.com. Retrieved 6 June 2011. <www.worldofbutterflies.com>

## Publishing the Paper

There are many ways you can publish or share your report. You can use a computer to write it and then give your teacher a copy of it. Another way to publish your report is to make a PowerPoint presentation to the class. You might make a brochure, depending on the subject. Or, you might create a poster using the information in the report.

# Test Yourself

**1** List three different types of visual aids you could use in a report about snakes.

_____

_____

_____

**2** List two ways you could publish your research report on a state.

_____

_____

**3** Which of these is the correct listing for a book in a bibliography?

   **A** Brady, Kyle. *My Life in Football.* New York: Sports Illustrated Books, 2011.

   **B** *My Life in Football.* Kyle Brady. Sports Illustrated Books, 2011.

   **C** *My Life in Football.* Sports Illustrated Books, New York, 2011.

   **D** New York: 2011. Sports Illustrated Books. Brady, Kyle. *My Life in Football.*

**4** Where would you find a bibliography in a report?

   **A** at the beginning

   **B** in the middle

   **C** at the end

   **D** before the table of contents

**5** Which would be a good choice to explain where the White House is located?

    **A** a chart

    **B** a diagram

    **C** a map of the United States

    **D** a street map of Washington, D.C.

**6** Which would you *most likely* find in a science report?

    **A** a map of a country

    **B** a diagram of a volcano

    **C** a photograph of children at a playground

    **D** a chart of students' favorite activities

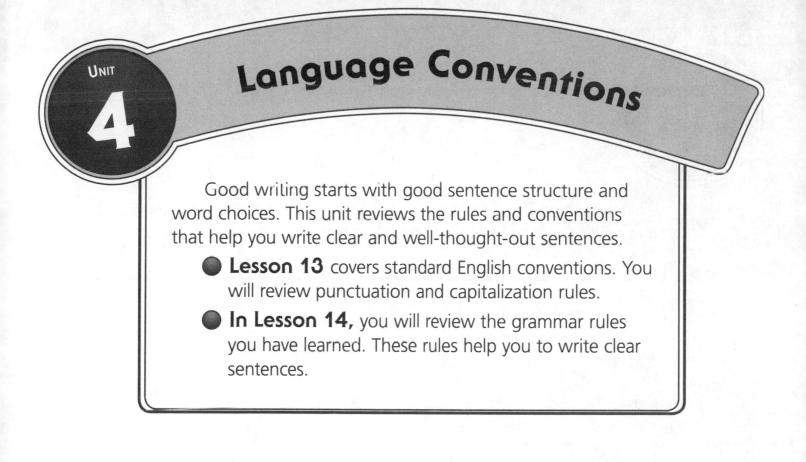

# UNIT 4

# Language Conventions

Good writing starts with good sentence structure and word choices. This unit reviews the rules and conventions that help you write clear and well-thought-out sentences.

- **Lesson 13** covers standard English conventions. You will review punctuation and capitalization rules.

- **In Lesson 14,** you will review the grammar rules you have learned. These rules help you to write clear sentences.

# Language Conventions

W.3.5, L.3.3

Understanding punctuation and capitalization is important. Following these rules makes you a better writer.

## Capitalization

The first word of a sentence always begins with a capital letter.

**Incorrect**    the gym teacher taught us to dance.
**Correct**    The gym teacher taught us to dance.

The names of people, places, days of the week, and months of the year also begin with capital letters.

| People | Places | Holidays |
|---|---|---|
| Lucy Fields | Eiffel Tower | Sunday |
| Rena Sanchez | Boston, Massachusetts | Thanksgiving Day |
| Jonathan Newhall | Downing Street | Memorial Day |

## Guided Practice

**Underline the word or words in each sentence that need a capital letter.**

i bought a tie for dad on saturday.

the tie was blue and yellow.

The team colors of fairmount college are blue and yellow.

✔ People, places, and days of the week are capitalized. The pronoun *I* is also capitalized. Here are the correct answers:

<u>i</u> bought a tie for <u>dad</u> on <u>saturday</u>.

<u>the</u> tie was blue and yellow.

The team colors of <u>fairmount college</u> are blue and yellow.

Titles of books, magazines, television shows, plays, and movies are capitalized. Quotation marks are used with the titles of plays, stories, and TV shows. Italics are used with the titles of books, magazines, and movies.

BOOK: *Charlie and the Chocolate Factory*
MAGAZINE: *Sports Illustrated for Kids*
TV SHOW: "Sesame Street"
PLAY: "Little Orphan Annie"
MOVIE: *Madagascar*

## Punctuation

A sentence begins with a capital letter and ends with a punctuation mark.

A sentence that makes a statement or gives a command ends with a **period.**

| | |
|---|---|
| **Statement** | Dogs like to run**.** |
| **Command** | Wait for your mother**.** |

A sentence that asks a question ends with a **question mark.**

**Question**      Did you finish your homework**?**

A sentence that express a strong feeling ends with an **exclamation mark.**

**Exclamation**   That was a funny show**!**

## Commas

A **comma** is used to separate the speaker and verbs such as *said, asked, answered,* and *exclaimed.* If the speaker comes before the quotation, a comma comes after the verb. Quotation marks are used to set off the words that are spoken.

Kevin said**,** "I'm over here."

A comma is used to separate the city and state in an address. It is also used to separate the street and the city.

143 Devon Road**,** Lemoyne**,** Maine
58 Beverly Drive**,** Springfield**,** Missouri

# Guided Practice

Did your grandmother help you write a letter to the mayor

I want to write a letter to him

Stop

428 Riverside Drive New York New York

> First, identify what type of sentence you are reading. Then you can decide on the correct punctuation. Here are the correct answers:

Did your grandmother help you write a letter to the mayor?

I want to write a letter to him.

Stop!

428 Riverside Drive, New York, New York

## Possessives

A possessive noun shows ownership. A noun can be made to show ownership by changing its form.

A photo of my **sister** is on the shelf. (noun)
My **sister's** photo is on the desk. (possessive noun)

To make a singular noun possessive add an apostrophe and an -*s*. A singular noun that ends in *s* still has an apostrophe and an -*s* added.

**Harry's** baseball mitt is on the table.
Mrs. **James's** roses are blooming.

To make a plural noun that ends in *s* possessive add an apostrophe only.

The **boys'** awards were on display.
The **Evans'** car is being repaired.

To make a plural noun that does not end in *s* a possessive noun, add an apostrophe and an *-s*.

The **children's** storybooks were in the basket.

Sometimes it is hard to tell if a word is a possessive noun or a plural noun just by hearing the word spoken. For example, *teachers*, *teacher's*, and *teachers'* all sound the same. However, by looking at the spelling of the word and the way the word is used in a sentence, you can determine what it is.

The **teachers** are meeting today. (plural noun)
The **teacher's** meeting is today. (singular possessive noun)
The **teachers'** meeting is today. (plural possessive noun)

## Guided Practice

**In each sentence, write the possessive form of the noun in parentheses on the line provided.**

The _____ barking was very loud. (dog)

The _____ scarf blew off in the wind. (man)

The _____ house is newly painted. (Peterses)

✓ Keep in mind whether the noun is singular or plural. Here are the correct answers:

The ____dog's____ barking was very loud. (dog)
The ____man's____ scarf blew off in the wind. (man)
The __Peterses'__ house is newly painted. (Peterses)

## Possessive Pronouns

Possessive pronouns are pronouns that show possession or ownership of something. Possessive pronouns replace nouns that show possession.

> Mitchell carried **Mitchell's** books. (possessive noun)
> Mitchell carried **his** books. (possessive pronoun)

Singular possessive nouns are *my, mine, your, yours, his, her, hers, its.*

> That is **his** coat.

Plural possessive nouns are *our, ours, your, yours, their, theirs.*

> Here is **your** pencil.

Some of these possessive pronouns are always used with nouns. These include *my, your, his, her, its, our, their.*

Other possessive pronouns always stand alone, which means nouns do not follow them. These include *mine, yours, his, hers, its, ours, theirs.*

> I think that notebook is **mine.**
> This is my blue jacket. **Hers** is on the chair.

## Guided Practice

**In each sentence, underline the possessive noun. On the line at the right, replace the possessive noun with the correct possessive pronoun.**

The winning design is Carol's and Ellie's. _____

The library's books are on the shelves. _____

He made chicken and rice for the children's dinner. _____

✔ Did you answer correctly? Here are the correct answers:

The winning design is <u>Carol's and Ellie's.</u>     _____theirs_____

The <u>library's</u> books are on the shelves.     _____Its_____

He made chicken and rice for the <u>children's</u> dinner. _____their_____

**UNIT 4** ▓▓▓▓▓▓▓▓▓▓▓▓▓▓▓▓▓▓▓▓▓▓▓▓▓▓▓▓▓▓▓▓▓▓▓▓▓▓▓▓▓
**178** Language Conventions

# Test Yourself

1 he loved the tie i bought for him.

2 I bought it in a store on rutherford avenue.

3 dad went to fairmount college and played football there.

**Add the correct punctuation to each sentence below.**

4 We need a new bicycle path

5 Did you ever have an accident on your bike

6 Wait for me

**Write the possessive noun of pronoun in each sentence.**

7 The _____ dinner was wonderful. (chef)

8 _____ coat is brand new. (Michael)

9 My _____ car is in the garage. (parents)

10

dad likes to watch Formula One racing. It's

fun to watch the race cars i like racing, too. My

favorite race car driver is rusty willis he is

from dad's hometown. he used to watch rusty at

the local track in stamford. now Rusty races in

a car called a Formula One. Does your father

like racing too maybe we can all watch a race

together sometime. there will be a race on

father's day that would be a great time to watch

together with our dads.

# Grammar

W.3.5, L.3.2

Grammar is an important part of writing. Understanding grammar rules will make you a better writer.

## Subject and Predicate

Every sentence has two parts: a **subject** and a **predicate.**

The subject tells who or what is doing the action in a sentence. The subject is usually the first part of a sentence.

The predicate tells what the subject does, is, had, or feels. The predicate is usually the second part of the sentence.

┌────── **Subject** ──────┬┬───── **Predicate** ─────┐
The children from my class <u>rushed into the room.</u>

A subject of a sentence is often a noun. See how each subject tells who or what is doing the action.

The <u>museum</u> opens today.
<u>People</u> are waiting in line.

Sometimes the subject of a sentence is a **pronoun.** A pronoun is a word that can take the place of a noun. When writing, it can help you avoid repeating words.

**Sue and Tim** are my friends.
**They** both live near me.

Here is a list of pronouns that can be used with subjects.

**Singular**
I, you, he, she, it

**Plural**
we, you, they

The predicate in a sentence is also called the **verb.** A verb usually shows action. It tells what the subject is doing. See how the verbs here tell what the cat is doing.

The cat **meows.**
The cat **plays** with yarn.

## Guided Practice

**Circle the subject. Underline the predicate. Then replace the subject with a subject pronoun.**

The wolves howl at night. _____

Kevin played the piano. _____

The children sang the song. _____

✓ The subject tells who or what is doing the action. The predicate shows the verb. A singular pronoun takes the place of a singular subject. Here are the correct answers:

(The wolves) <u>howl at night.</u>    _____They_____

(Kevin) <u>played the piano.</u>    _____He_____

(The children) <u>sang the song.</u>    _____They_____

## Singular and Plural Nouns _____

A singular noun is one person, place, or thing. A plural noun is more than one person, place, or thing. Usually, plural nouns add in *s*.

| Singular Noun | Plural Noun |
| --- | --- |
| club | clubs |
| basket | baskets |
| girl | girls |
| school | schools |

Nouns that end in *s, ch, sh, x,* or *z* add *-es* to show they are plural.

| Singular Noun | Plural Noun |
| --- | --- |
| box | boxes |
| church | churches |
| dress | dresses |
| wish | wishes |

There are some plural nouns that do not end in *s*. These are called **irregular plural nouns.** Here are some examples of irregular plural nouns:

| Singular Noun | Plural Noun |
|---|---|
| child | children |
| goose | geese |
| foot | feet |
| mouse | mice |
| ox | oxen |

## Guided Practice

**Decide whether each noun is singular or plural. Next, to each word write an S for singular or a P for plural.**

salamandars _____

women _____

cupcake _____

football _____

Singular means "one." Plural is "more than one." Here are the correct answers:

salamandars _____P_____

women _____P_____

cupcake _____S_____

football _____S_____

## Subject and Verb Agreement _____

Every complete sentence has a subject and a predicate. The predicate is a verb. Sometimes the verb is in the present tense. A present-tense verb tells what is happening now or what keeps on happening.

For a sentence to be correct, the subject and verb must agree in number. That means that if the subject is singular, the verb must be singular. Remember that singular means "one." Read each sentence below. The subject is underlined. The verb is italic. Notice the endings on the verbs.

### Singular Subject-Verb Agreement
<u>Harry</u> *eats* a sandwich each day. (ending *s*)
My <u>cat</u> *watches* birds. (ending *es*)
Each <u>player</u> *takes* a turn. (ending *s*)

The subject nouns *Harry, cat,* and *player* are all singular. They need singular verbs. Usually, singular verbs in the present tense end in *s* or *es*.

Plural verbs in the present tense do not end in *s* or *es*. If the subject is plural, the verb must be plural. Remember that plural means "more than one."

Notice how the noun and the verb in each sentence below go together. This means that they agree in number. The subject is underlined. The verb is in italic.

### Plural Subject-Verb Agreement
The <u>sisters</u> *share* their clothes.
<u>Families</u> *work* together to clean the park.
The <u>students</u> *raise* money every year.

The sentences below show correct agreement in number. The subject in each sentence is underlined. The verb is italic. Notice the endings on the singular verbs.

| | |
|---|---|
| **Singular** | The <u>girl</u> *throws* the ball. |
| **Plural** | Those <u>girls</u> *throw* hard. |
| **Singular** | Each <u>child</u> *chooses* a party favor. |
| **Plural** | The <u>children</u> *choose* their party favors. |

Sometimes nouns joined by *and* form a **compound subject.** A compound subject is plural. The verb must be plural, too.

<u>Alisha and Ben</u> *like* pizza.     <u>Your socks and shoes</u> *are* here.

**UNIT 4**
Language Conventions

# Guided Practice

My sister _____ her puppy today. (choose)

Meg _____ to call her puppy Daisy. (want)

Daisy and the other puppies _____ all day. (play)

Our parents _____ one puppy is enough! (think)

✓ The subject and verb should agree in number. A singular subject takes a singular verb. A compound subject is plural. It takes a plural verb. Here are the correct answers:

My sister ___*chooses*___ her puppy today. (choose)

Meg ___*wants*___ to call her puppy Daisy. (want)

Daisy and the other puppies ___*play*___ all day. (play)

Our parents ___*think*___ one puppy is enough! (think)

## Verb Tenses

A verb in the **present tense** tells what is happening now or what keeps on happening. A verb in the **past tense** tells what happened before, or in the past.

Read each pair of sentences below. The verbs are underlined. Notice the ending *ed* is added to each past-tense verb. Most verbs form the past tense with *ed*.

**Present Tense**    Fresh bread smells wonderful.
**Past Tense**        Yesterday, the bread smelled wonderful.

**Present Tense**    My brothers skate once a week.
**Past Tense**        Last week, my brothers skated twice.

**Present Tense**    Bees hum in the garden.
**Past Tense**        Bees hummed in the garden

# Forms of *be*

The verb *be* is irregular. It changes to a different word for the past tense. The form of the verb must also match the subject. This chart shows when to use different forms of the verb *be*.

| Subject | Present Tense | Past Tense |
|---|---|---|
| **Singular Pronouns** | | |
| I | am | was |
| you | are | were |
| he, she, it | is | was |
| **Plural Pronouns** | | |
| we | are | were |
| they | are | were |
| **Singular Nouns** | is | was |
| **Plural Nouns** | are | were |

# Irregular Verbs

The past tense of most verbs is formed by adding *-ed*. Some verbs have a different spelling and sound in the past tense. This chart shows some irregular verbs that are used often.

**Irregular Verbs**

| Present Tense | Past Tense |
|---|---|
| bring | brought |
| come | came |
| eat | ate |
| fly | flew |
| has, have | had |
| give | gave |
| say | said |
| take | took |
| write | wrote |

# Guided Practice

Tim flew the plane over our house.　＿＿＿＿＿＿＿＿＿＿

My dad likes cream in his coffee.　＿＿＿＿＿＿＿＿＿＿

The two cats were under the couch.　＿＿＿＿＿＿＿＿＿＿

✔ Present-tense verbs tell what is happening now. Past-tense verbs tell what happened before. Here are the correct answers:

Tim <u>flew</u> the plane over our house.　＿＿＿_past_＿＿＿

My dad <u>likes</u> cream in his coffee.　＿＿_present_＿＿

The two cats <u>were</u> under the couch.　＿＿_past_＿＿

## Adjectives

Words that describe a person, animal, place, or thing are called **adjectives.** Adjectives answer these questions: How many? How much? What kind?

Adjectives can be used to compare two or more things.

old　　　old<u>er</u>　　　old<u>est</u>

The **comparative** is when you compare two things. Add -er or -r to a one syllable word to compare two things. Use *more* instead of an ending for words with more than one syllable.

bigg<u>er</u>　　　small<u>er</u>　　　<u>more</u> intelligent

The **superlative** is when you compare three or more things. Add -est or -st to a one syllable word to compare three or more things. Use *most* instead of an ending for words with more than one syllable.

bigg<u>est</u>　　　small<u>est</u>　　　<u>most</u> intelligent

# Guided Practice

**Write the comparative and superlative forms of the adjectives.**

heavy    _____    _____

sweet    _____    _____

kind    _____    _____

> ✓ The comparative is when you add *-er* to an adjective. The superlative is when you add *-est* to an adjective. Here are the correct answers:

heavy    <u>heavier</u>    <u>heaviest</u>

sweet    <u>sweeter</u>    <u>sweetest</u>

kind    <u>kinder</u>    <u>kindest</u>

## Conjunctions

**Conjunctions** are connecting words. They connect other words or groups of words.

**Coordinating conjunctions** join two words or groups of words that are equally important. These are conjunctions like: *for, and, nor, or, but, yet, so.*

> Kevin and Ricky are going to the store *so* they can buy school supplies.

**Subordinating conjunctions** connect groups of words that do not have the same importance. Subordinate means "less important." The group of words that follow the subordinate conjunction are less important. They need another group of words for their meaning to be clear. These are words like: *before, after, when, since, because, while, if, unless, even.*

> He did not look for the book *because* he knew where it was.

These conjunctions help make different types of sentences.

A **simple sentence** has a subject and a predicate.

> Grace likes to roller skate.

A **compound sentence** has two sentences made into one. The coordinating conjunctions *and, or,* and *but* are used in a compound sentence.

> Grace likes to roller skate *and* she likes to ice skate.

A **complex sentence** is two sentences connected with subordinating conjunctions. These are the words *because, although, while, after, if,* and *until.*

> *Although* Grace likes to roller skate, she doesn't always have time to do it.

## Guided Practice

**Identify the conjunction. Write coordinating or subordinate on the line.**

Lori put on her shoes and opened the door. _____

If you look, you will see two presents. _____

She swam quickly, but she still lost the race. _____

One was tall while the other was short. _____

✓ A coordinating conjunction joins two words or groups of words that are equal. A subordinate joins two groups of words that are unequal. One group needs the other to make sense. Here are the correct answers:

Lori put on her shoes <u>and</u> opened the door. _coordinating_

<u>If</u> you look, you will see two presents. _subordinate_

She swam quickly, <u>but</u> she still lost the race. _coordinating_

One was tall <u>while</u> the other was short. _subordinate_

# Adverbs

A word that describes a verb is called an **adverb**. An adverb may answer the questions: How? How often? Where? When?

Ilana answered **correctly.** (tells **how** she answered)
It rains **frequently** in spring. (tells **how often** it rains)
I looked **everywhere** for you. (tells **where** I looked)
**Finally,** the actors bowed. (tells **when** the actors bowed)

Many adverbs are made by adding -*ly* to an adjective.

## Guided Practice

**Write an adverb on the line.**

"I can solve your problem," said Owl _____.

Zachary _____ snapped his fingers.

I see that you have completed your work _____.

✓ **Adverbs describe the verb. Here is a sample answer:**

"I can solve your problem," said Owl ___*knowingly*___.

Zachary ___*loudly*___ snapped his fingers.

I see that you have completed your work ___*quickly*___.

**UNIT 4** ❊❊❊❊❊❊❊❊❊❊❊❊❊❊❊❊❊❊❊❊❊❊❊❊❊❊❊❊❊❊
Language Conventions

# Test Yourself

**1** The new car is in the garage. _____

**2** Abbey and John laughed. _____

**3** Jill spoke to the reporter. _____

**4** The trees grew a lot this spring. _____

**5** The birds sing so sweetly. _____

**Decide whether each noun is singular or plural. Next, to each word write an S for singular or a P for plural.**

**6** keyboard _____

**7** race cars _____

**8** classrooms _____

**9** school _____

**Read the paragraph. Find the four verbs that are incorrect. Write the present-form tense for each one on the lines.**

Jake and his twin sister likes the field behind their school. Every day they plays games there. Jake really enjoy the soccer matches. Of all his classmates, he and his sister run the fastest around the track. Only his dog Willie beat them.

10 _____

11 _____

12 _____

13 _____

**Write an adverb on the line.**

14 To win the game, the teammates must play _____.

15 Sara climbed into bed and _____ fell asleep.

16 The wind blew _____ and toppled trees.

**17** Edit the paragraphs below. Cross out each mistake, and write the corrections above it.

My family move to a new home last November. My brother and I brother worried about starting a new school. We be twins. He and I wanted to be in the same class. We was sent to different classes. If I'm scared, my heart beat fast. It were beating like a drum!

My new teacher was Ms. Gerald. She smiled at me and say, "Welcome to our school. We're happy your here." I looked at my new classmates. All of they were clapping to welcome me. Six months has passed since then. Wagner School feel like home to me. My brother agree. We both look forward to next year.

**18** Edit the paragraphs below. Cross out each mistake and write the corrections above it.

Last summer I go to day camp for the first time. Camp monroe was fun but it also gave me a chance to learn. Something important. I learn how to swim.

The beginning swimmers was called the Tadpoles. My friend Aaron and I and five other kids was all Tadpoles. our swimming teacher was named pat. First, we blowed bubbles in the pool. Then we kicked our foots to make big splashes. Next, Pat drop a coin into the pool and it sank to the bottom. We had to open our eyes underwater. To find the coin and pick them up. I try three times until I finally picked up the coin. I brang it proud to Pat.

After that, pat showed us the crawl. You has to turn your head to breathe in and blow out. You must also pull strong with each arm. And kick steady. The crawl take practice.

At last, I swimmed from one end of the pool to the other. Im going back to camp next summer but I won't be a Tadpole. Ill be swimming with the Sharks

**UNIT 4** ▓▓▓▓▓▓▓▓▓▓▓▓▓▓▓▓▓▓▓▓▓▓▓▓▓▓▓▓▓▓▓▓▓▓▓▓▓
Language Conventions

# PRACTICE TEST

## Important Events in the Life of Dr. Sally Ride

**1951**

Sally Kristen Ride is born in Los Angeles, California. As a child, she plays tennis and likes to look through telescopes at the stars and planets.

**1968**

Sally Ride graduates from Westlake High School in Los Angeles. Her favorite things to study are math and science. She is a champion tennis player, but she decides to give up tennis and go to college.

**1973**

Sally Ride graduates from Stanford University, where she has studied English and physics.

**1975**

Sally Ride gets her master's degree in science from Stanford.

**1978**

Sally Ride becomes Dr. Sally Ride when she gets her doctorate in science from Stanford. In the same year, Sally Ride becomes an astronaut for NASA.

**1982**

Sally Ride is chosen to be the first American woman in space.

**1983**
Sally Ride flies into space for the first time. She is a member of the Challenger crew. The Challenger launches from Kennedy Space Center in Florida. It orbits Earth for six days.

**1984**
Sally Ride flies into space a second time with four other astronauts and two scientists.

**1986**
Ride's third flight into space is cancelled because of the Challenger explosion. This accident kills all of the astronauts on board. Dr. Ride is asked to help find out why the accident happened. Sally Ride writes a children's book called *To Space and Back*. This book describes her experiences in space.

**1989**
Sally Ride begins teaching physics at the University of California in San Diego.

**2001**
Sally Ride starts a company that helps young girls learn science. Dr. Ride is the president of the company. She is a role model for girls who want to study science. Her mission is to have more girls become scientists.

**2012**
Sally Ride dies on July 23.

**1** What is Sally Ride famous for?

_____

_____

_____

_____

**2** Why did Sally Ride give up playing tennis?

_____

_____

_____

_____

**Practice Test**

**3** Read this question. Then plan, write, revise, and edit your
answer on the pages that follow.

> Your teacher has asked you to write a report about
> Dr. Sally Ride. Write one or more paragraphs that tell
> what Dr. Ride did. Tell why she is an important woman in
> history.
>
> In your response be sure to:
>
> • include a topic sentence and a main idea
>
> • use connecting words
>
> • put events in the right time order

## Prewriting

Underline or mark up the question as you wish. Then use the
rest of this page to plan your answer. Choose a graphic organizer
to plan your answer.

_____

_____

_____

_____

_____

_____

_____

_____

_____

# Drafting

Use this page to write your draft.

_____

_____

_____

_____

_____

_____

_____

_____

_____

_____

_____

_____

_____

_____

_____

_____

**Practice Test**

# Revising and Editing

Use this page to make your revisions. Then edit your work.

_____

_____

_____

_____

_____

_____

_____

_____

_____

_____

_____

_____

_____

_____

_____

_____

_____

**Revising and Editing**

# Publish

Write your final copy on the page below. Then show it to your teacher.

## Using Capital Letters

- Begin every sentence with a capital letter: **M**y bike is green.

- Begin each part of a person's name with a capital letter. Include titles that are used as part of the name.

    **R**yan **W. C**ooper      **A**unt **R**osa

    **P**resident **A**dams      **D**r. **C**hen

- Begin words that name days, months, holidays, and places with a capital letter.

    **M**onday      **O**ctober      **F**lag **D**ay

    **R**iverside **S**chool      **N**ew **Y**ork **C**ity

- Do NOT begin the names of seasons with a capital letter.

    winter      fall      spring      summer

## Using Punctuation Marks
### End Marks

- End every sentence with a period (**.**), a question mark (**?**), or an exclamation point (**!**).

- End a statement with a period: Tadpoles turn into frogs**.**

- End a question with a question mark: Where is your jacket**?**

- End an exclamation with an exclamation point: I love summer**!**

## Commas (,)

- When two sentences are joined by *and, but,* or *or,* use a comma before the joining word.

    Tyler played checkers, **and** Elizabeth read a book.

- Use commas between words that name things in a group.

    Mix together the flour, sugar, salt, and oil.

- Use a comma between the day and year in a date.

    April 7, 2011

- Use a comma between a city and state.

    Omaha, Nebraska

## Apostrophes (')

- Use an apostrophe to show who owns or has something. If the owner is singular (one person or thing), add an apostrophe and -*s.*

    Matt**'s** dad          a duck**'s** beak

- If the owner is plural (more than one) and ends in *s,* add just an apostrophe.

    three girl**s'** scores          all the cat**s'** tails

- Use an apostrophe to show where letters are missing in a contraction.

    I + am = I'm (*a* is missing)
    is + not = isn't (*o* is missing)

## Quotation Marks (" ")

- Use quotation marks before and after the words a person says.

    Jessica said, "I will play my violin."

**Handbook**

## Titles

- Capitalize the first word, last word, and every important word in a title.

- Underline book titles.

     book: <u>**T**he **W**ind in the **W**illows</u> (underline)

- Use quotation marks for shorter works, such as poems and articles.

     poem: **"T**he **O**wl and the **P**ussycat**"**

     article: **"T**ips for **S**afe **B**iking**"**

# Using Correct Grammar
## Subject-Verb Agreement

- When you use an action verb in the present tense, add *-s* or *-es* to the verb if the subject is a singular noun (one person or thing). Do not add *-s* or *-es* to the verb if the subject is plural (more than one).

     Emily sing**s**      children sing      Carlos and Becky sing

- If the subject is a pronoun, add *-s* or *-es* to the verb only if the pronoun is *he, she,* or *it.*

     he eat**s**      I eat      you eat      we eat      they eat

## Subject-Verb Agreement with Forms of *be*

- If the subject is a singular noun (one person or thing), use *is* for the present tense and *was* for the past tense.

     Kayla **is**      the sky **was**

- If the subject is a plural noun or more than one noun, use *are* for the present tense and *were* for the past tense.

     Wrong: the pencils **is**      Wrong: the pen and pencil **was**

     Correct: the pencils **are**      Correct: the pen and pencil **were**

- Use the correct form of *be* with a singular or plural pronoun subject.

| Present Tense | | Past Tense | |
|---|---|---|---|
| Singular | Plural | Singular | Plural |
| I **am** | we **are** | I **was** | we **were** |
| you **are** | you **are** | you **were** | you **were** |
| he, she, *or* it **is** | they **are** | he, she, *or* it **was** | they **were** |

## Irregular Verbs

Many past tense verbs do not end in *ed.* It will help to learn the correct forms by heart.

| Present | Past | Past Participle |
|---|---|---|
| is | was | (has) been |
| begin | began | (has) begun |
| bring | brought | (has) brought |
| choose | chose | (has) chosen |
| come | came | (has) come |
| go | went | (has) gone |
| have | had | (has) had |
| know | knew | (has) known |
| make | made | (has) made |
| run | ran | (has) run |
| say | said | (has) said |
| take | took | (has) taken |
| write | wrote | (has) written |

## Subject and Object Pronouns

- Pronouns have different subject and object forms.

- Use subject pronouns as the subject of a sentence.

- Use object pronouns after an action verb.

| Subject | Object |
|---------|--------|
| I | me |
| he | him |
| she | her |
| we | us |
| they | them |

**Subject Pronoun**

Wrong: Julia and **me** worked.
Correct: Julia and **I** worked.

**Object Pronoun**

Wrong: Joe helped Julia and **I**.
Correct: Joe helped Julia and **me**.

## Naming Yourself Last

- When you speak of yourself and another person, name yourself last.

    **Luis** and **I** are friends.        Save seats for **Shelby** and **me.**

## Tricky Words

- Some words are often confused. Remember to use these words correctly.

| a/an | Use *a* before a consonant sound.<br>Use *an* before a vowel sound.<br>   Wrong: **a** elephant     Correct: **an** elephant |
|---|---|
| have/of | Use *have* or *'ve* after words such as *could, should,* and *would.* Do not use *of.*<br>   Wrong: We should **of** won.<br>   Correct: We should **have** won. We should**'ve** won. |
| hear/here | *Hear* means "to be aware of sound":  I **hear** tapping.<br>(TIP: the word *hear* contains *ear!*)<br>*Here* means "in this place": Sit right **here.** |
| its/it's | *Its* means "belonging to it": The cat licked **its** fur.<br>*It's* means "it is": **It's** Tuesday. |
| than/then | *Than* is a word for comparing:<br>   Eric is taller **than** Tim.<br>*Then* means "at that time" or "next":<br>   What happened **then?** |
| their/<br>there/<br>they're | *Their* means "belonging to them": **Their** team lost.<br>*There* means "in that place": Put the box **there.**<br>*They're* means "they are": **They're** going home. |
| who's/<br>whose | *Who's* means "who is": **Who's** knocking?<br>Use *whose* to ask or tell about the owner of something: **Whose** dog is that? I know **whose** it is. |
| your/<br>you're | *Your* means "belonging to you": Tie **your** sneaker.<br>*You're* means "you are": **You're** very kind. |

## Proofreading Symbols

| Symbol | Meaning | Example |
|---|---|---|
| ∧ | Add letters or words. | This game is played ∧ a computer. (^on^) |
| ⊙ | Add a period. | These cards are for the board game⊙ |
| ≡ | Capitalize a letter. | ≡you can practice a lot. |
| ∧̇ | Add a comma. | We brought the game, some food∧and balloons. |
| ℐ | Take out letters or words. | You have the ~~board and~~ game. |
| ∼ | Switch the position of letters or words. | Use the (red⁀large) pieces. |

# Notes